D1201874

I Hate to Make Speeches--
Help for People Who Must

I Hate to Make Speeches-- Help for People Who Must

John Quick

Drawings by Larry Kirby

GROSSET & DUNLAP
A National General Company
Publishers   New York

Copyright © 1973 by John Quick
All rights reserved
Published simultaneously in Canada
Library of Congress Catalog Card Number: 72-90833
ISBN: 0-448-01793-8

First Printing

Printed in the United States of America

*This book is dedicated to
my daughter, Margaret.*

*It is also written in
memory of General George
Armstrong Custer (1839–1876).
Let his last engagement
serve as a reminder to you.
Learn something about your
audience.*

Contents

Preface

If there is a chance that you will ever have to get up there in front of everybody and talk to them with your mouth, this book is intended for *you*.

(The publishers made me say that. They're afraid you'll pick this book up and think it's a business book and won't buy it. But they're just as afraid that you might be a businessman and *not* buy it because you think it *isn't* a business book. So the answer is "No, it isn't" to some of you, and "Yes, it is" to others. [The publishers and I also got into a hassle about the title of this book. I wanted to call it *The Battle of the Little Bigmouth,* but they were afraid you'd think it was a book about Indians.])

Anyway, here's a list of people who will be able to use the book:

1. Brand-new teachers
2. New (and used) politicians

3. Students
4. Candidates for almost anything
5. People who speak at town meetings
6. The Silent Majority
7. Military people who make briefings
8. Lawyers new to trial work
9. Anybody concerned with the manufacturing, marketing, or distribution of a product
10. Conservatives
11. Businessmen on The Way Up
12. Radicals
13. Dictators in small countries everywhere
14. WASPS
15. Anybody connected with the government
16. Grand juries
17. Minorities of all sorts
18. Almost everybody else, including dentists, consultants, salesmen, parachutists, hookers, Californians, and persons who commute into Manhattan by train or bus

Thank you.

I Hate to Make Speeches--Help for People Who Must

Introduction

I'm going to prove something to you.

To show that I really know something about communications I'm going to tell you four things, at least one of which you will remember for ten years. I *guarantee* it. If you forget all four of them I'll give you $400.00. That's $100.00 apiece.

Here they are.

1. Every time you see a new moon you will notice its similarity to a toenail clipping.

2. Dead people develop purple bruises on whatever part of their body they're lying on because gravity pulls the blood there.

3. You can get chewing gum out of your hair by rubbing peanut butter on it.

4. You can stop a charging lion by waiting until he's practically on top of you and then spitting in his mouth.

I'll tell you where I got these facts.

1. I was in Colorado one time when my friend Bob Rechnitz pointed at the sky and said, "I'm going to tell you something you will never forget. You see that new moon? It looks like a toenail clipping. Every time you see a new moon from now on you'll remember what I told you." (Later I passed this fact along to a poetry-oriented person who replied, "No, I *won't* remember that. But I'll do something else. From now on when I look at my toenails I'll see a new moon.")

2. In *The Andromeda Strain,* Dr. Crichton says that dead people get big bruises where they're lying. Because he's a doctor I tend to regard this as a fact. It is a marvelous, morbid piece of information to have.

3. I was listening to the car radio one day and heard somebody say that peanut butter, because of the oil in it, would soften chewing gum so that you could get it out of your hair. (Shampooing will then remove the peanut butter.) In this way you would avoid having to cut off a big glob of hair.

The new moon
looks like
a toenail clipping.

I hope this information is true because I continue to remember it and may have to try it some day.

4. A long time ago I heard that you could turn a lion's charge by spitting in his mouth because lions are really disgusted by human saliva. This is a nice last-ditch piece of information to have. (And even if it doesn't work, think of how you'll be remembered by onlookers: "Yes," they will say, "I was there when Dave got his head bitten off by the lion. It was the bravest thing I ever saw. He stood his ground and died like a man.")

You can turn
a lion's charge
by
spitting in his mouth.

So far in this introduction I've done a few of the key things that a presentation is supposed to do. I've gotten your immediate attention. I've talked to you in language you could understand. I've communicated ideas in a way you will remember for a long time. I may even have committed you to some future course of action. You may try to remove some chewing gum at some point, or stop a lion.

1. The Author's Career with His Mouth, Etc.

I don't know why I started appearing in front of audiences in the first place. As nearly as I can remember, the process has always scared me to death.

One of my earliest recollections is standing in a woodshed in a small Oregon town trying to memorize the lines for a pageant. I remember looking at the sky and saying aloud, "If I ever get through this one, I'll never do it again." That night I was moderately triumphant in three speaking parts (and three costume changes). I played a black cat, a brownie, and the minute hand of a clock.

From that point forward I persisted in the idea that it was somehow an All Right thing to do, because it entertained people, or it entertained me, or something.

7

This led to a shaky, on-off, and finally abortive attempt at being an actor—an exercise that took the better part of eight years. In a couple of colleges I worked in shoebox theaters, children's theaters, tents, in the round, and in basements. I worked in summer-stock companies, in companies that moved by truck, and companies that moved by airplane. In the service I ran a small radio station, and later I worked as a comedian in loud, drunk little West Coast nightclubs. Toward the end I did live television in Denver—as a small-time sheriff on a children's show and as a hillbilly on a western variety show. All told, I think I earned about $181.00.

Besides gaining an insight into the meaning of poverty, I learned a few other things from the experience.

The main thing is this: even with speakers or entertainers who are accustomed to being in front of people, things can always go seriously wrong. Sets fall down, lights explode, and zippers unzip. Or people get overconfident. Or they get so wound up in what they're doing they forget the audience. A great many theatrical groups, professional and otherwise, fail for the simple reason that they forget about the audience and tend to concentrate on the process of doing "theater." While involved in all this artistry they fail to remember that their play has to be publicized somehow, that tickets have to be sold, that orange juice has to be served between acts, that cars have to be parked someplace, and that rest rooms have to be provided for the audience.

The problem can become even worse when people start doing "drama" exclusively, and find some *new* ways of cutting themselves off from the audience. I've worked with some self-proclaimed "method" actors who became so involved in their characters that they forgot about the needs of the audience to either see or hear them.

Having worked mostly in comedy, I never had that particular problem. Comedy, when played live, depends exclusively on listening to an audience and adjusting the pace and tempo to what *it* needs. It's possible to slow down a little when things are going well, or accelerate when things are going to hell.

I got another very valuable thing from this training that helped later in business presentations or any other public appearance. It embarrassed me quite a bit at first, but I got over it. One of the first classes an actor has to take is a cross between calisthenics and ballet. The year-long course I took was called Rhythmic and Dramatic Movement. It sounds very sweet, but I don't recall anything in military basic training that was half as bad as some of the exercises in that class. The net effect of all the miserable exercises and the arm and leg waving was that we could, thenceforth, walk across a stage with a fair chance of not falling over the furniture or knocking down a set. We could move around on the stage and look fairly natural. It began to answer the question of "What do I do with my hands? (Or my arms, legs, feet, and body?)"

Another thing about theater was learning about long rehearsals.

And I also learned that the process of "looking good" on a stage is a very complicated business, and altogether artificial. Somebody (and his staff) has to worry a great deal about the background setting you work against. Somebody else, with another staff, worries about costumes that will work for you, for the play, and *with* the setting. The right props have to be found. Makeup has to be planned and applied properly. Lighting has to be

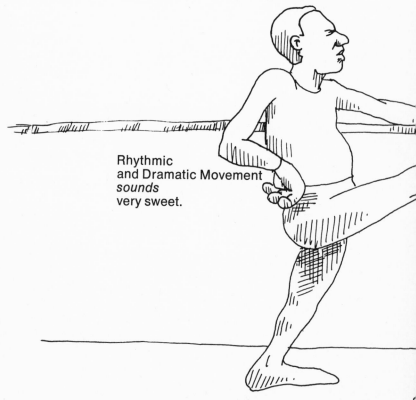

Rhythmic
and Dramatic Movement
sounds
very sweet.

developed with the needs of the play in mind, but also in consideration of the sets, the costumes, and the makeup. The actors have to rehearse, not only to remember lines, but to be able to speak them as though they were being spoken for the first time. The director is at the top of everything. He controls it all—the people onstage and off, the appearance of everything, and the needs of the play in terms of the content, continuity, and pace of the material.

Even when all of these aspects are carefully coordi-

nated and executed by professionals, shows still fail. They simply fail to "work."

Now, compare *that* sort of careful effort to your own attempts at being a speaker in front of a group.

Chances are you haven't rehearsed. You have no specialized lighting. There is little concern for costume or how you will look. You don't appear in front of a set. You very often have little concern for the audience and what they want or need—and little, if any, information on what it's going to be like up there in front of them.

But all of us, in our daydreams, are spellbinders. Courtroom defense attorneys. Speakers who can mesmerize any audience. These daydreams are often so real that we make remarks like, "Things will be O.K.; I'll just get up there and wing it."

When the chips are finally down, however, the story is quite different. You're all alone. You don't really know what you're doing. Your armpits are soaked. Your stomach doesn't feel good. And your knees tremble. You still have a shred of confidence left, though. You pin all your hopes on your mouth.

And then it opens. A thin, reedy, Donald Duck voice comes out. Or a coughing fit. Or a string of "uh's" and "uhm's" so prolonged that people begin to wonder if you're going to do the whole presentation in Morse code.

It's a million laughs.

2. Trying to Help Others with *Their* Mouths

After the experience with theater and live television (and shots at career opportunities as a fry cook, shrubbery salesman, bellhop, and teletype operator), I infiltrated U.S. industry and somehow became an industrial motion picture producer. One of the things that seemed very reasonable about motion pictures was that if you ever succeeded in doing something right, you would have a permanent record of it. You could also exercise some control over the content of the material, the way in which the content was strung together, and the speed with which the information was presented.

I discovered that while this was theoretically true there are pitfalls, mechanical and otherwise. Some of

them have to do with weather and the statistical im-
probabilities of going seventeen days with no sunshine.
Other problems arise when you load film magazines
backward, forget to bring the battery for the camera
motor, or drop the entire camera out of an airplane.
One of the biggest thrills, however, is to sucessfully
accomplish all the photography and then get a call from
the laboratory telling you that something incredible has
happened. Such as a "slight scratch" on "part" of the
film—which translates eventually as a ¼-inch gouge
down the center of 2,700 feet of original. I remember

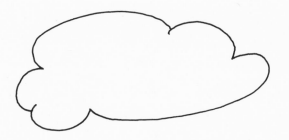

There are
certain pitfalls
in movie
production.

one conversation that began, "Listen, I know how fantastic this is going to sound to you . . . the idea that a film processor could catch *fire*. . . ."

But all of those details aside, the biggest single problem of film is the same as that of a face-to-face meeting with a group—*too many words,* and *too much detail.*

I then got involved in advertising and promotion. I saw this as the ultimate communications challenge— using short bursts of words and pictures, and influencing people by getting immediately to the point.

During this period I spent an interlude in New York,

doing presentations for advertising agencies and other clients. In many cases we were involved in the design, development, and production of an entire presentation. Sometimes we only produced visuals.

It came as a big surprise to me to learn that New York advertising agencies (supposedly the Slickest Communicators Anywhere) were capable of mounting spectacularly dull presentations. The main reason for failure was one of the most common worldwide—too many people simultaneously trying to be in charge. But that's an administrative problem, and I leave it to behavioral scientists.

Let me tell you about some purely *mechanical* problems.

In one classic instance all I had to do was "take care of the little details for somebody doing a twenty-minute presentation at the Plaza Hotel." I would like to describe this event in considerable detail, because it illustrates a few of the problems that come up when you make an all-out effort to produce something that is supposed to look easy, comfortable, and relaxed.

The client was interested in showing a large group of tourist agency people some information about an area of the Mediterranean. The audience was already assembled for a convention, so it was decided that a buffet breakfast and a short presentation would be easiest to handle. The client cheerfully added that I could use their projector. That conversation took place on Wednesday afternoon. The presentation was scheduled for Friday morning.

Arrangements had been made to use the grand ballroom of the Plaza because the expected audience would number two or three hundred. I looked at the room and discovered that the distance from the screen to an alcove where I could stick a projector was about eighty feet. At such a distance it is no longer possible to use unmodified home projectors.

I also discovered that it was more than simply a matter of *one* projector. In addition to 35mm slides, there was also a portion of a filmstrip, and some TV commercials on 16mm film. Doing the job successfully required the use of four projectors, and four uncommon projectors at that. They would need special light sources to project a bright picture over such a long distance.

Thursday morning I was on hand with two Plaza Hotel electricians and a consulting engineer from a New York audiovisual equipment rental company.

It was simple. We needed two Carousel projectors with custom-made xenon light sources and a heavy-duty dissolve unit to go back and forth between the two 35mm projectors. We needed a 16mm projector with a xenon light source. And we needed a filmstrip projector with a xenon light source. Each projector, regardless of format, required a lens of a certain focal length in order to fill the screen. When we found the right lenses we discovered that the Plaza's screen wasn't quite the right size for our purposes, and so we brought in another one. A bigger one.

The 16mm film had a sound track, the output of which had to go into a special amplifier. The amplifier needed was different from that required by the Plaza's sound system; that meant we had to get a completely separate one, including different speakers.

So we put a couple of speakers on the stage and ran their cables back to the amplifier for eighty feet. The 16mm projector worked like a champ.

The filmstrip projector (which plays an LP record) didn't work like a champ. It didn't work at all. The engineer called in an assistant.

I, meanwhile, investigated the problem of the client's using the Plaza's microphone and PA system in conjunction with *our* sound system, but ours caused a feedback problem. (Microphone feedback is that wonderful dying-pig noise.)

We decided, therefore, to have the speaker's microphone go through our own sound system. That would simplify things. So we found a compatible microphone and ran its mike cable the eighty feet back to the amplifier. (This process, called learning-as-you-go-along, necessitated numerous urgent calls to the equipment rental company for some new item to be delivered. They were thrilled.)

Five P.M. came. The filmstrip sound system problem was solved, but the speaker's microphone developed a loud buzz. The alcove in the back of the ballroom was starting to fill up with cables.

A friend dropped in and foolishly asked if he could help. I said, "Sure." I think he might have meant to stay for fifteen minutes. He was there until midnight and returned for two hours the following day.

At about 6:00 P.M. it occurred to somebody that the speaker was supposed to advance the 35mm slides as he narrated them. This happens all the time, so remote cables are made for Carousel projectors. It works out, however, that very few ninety-foot remote cables are around at any given moment.

A man was dispatched to find one or build one. We simultaneously cured the microphone buzz, but developed a hum in the 16mm projector.

Evening, as they say, fell on Gotham.

We began to address the problem (the simple problem) of the compound movement that takes place when you (1) bring down the house lights and (2) bring up the stage lights. This isn't a particularly difficult thing to do, and it looks nice. Much better than cutting house lights (and being plunged in darkness) and then snapping on the stage lights. This is too abrupt and painful. You want the house lights to dim gradually, and simultaneously have stage lights appear on the speaker (actor, talent, or whatever you want to call him). The audience is then able to shift its attention very easily from the room and the crowd to the person on the stage. As the lights dim, the audience prepares to listen and watch.

We faced only two small problems at the Plaza. The dimmers were at the other end of the room from us, and the lights weren't set up yet.

By 11:00 P.M. all the necessary electrical work had been traced, checked, fixed, and tested. We had eliminated the last of the hums, buzzes, shrieks, and clicks. The lights worked.

By way of a final rehearsal we tested everything in the order it was supposed to be used. The 16mm film broke.

Sixteen-mm film is easy to splice. All you need is a splicer and some film cement. Plaza room service can do a lot of marvelous things, but they can't be expected to provide 16mm film splicers. I called anyway.

The equipment company had splicers. The engineer worked for the equipment company, but he didn't have his key. So he called somebody who did. As these events unfolded I missed the last train to Chappaqua.

The splicer arrived and my friend decided to leave. With him went the engineer, the engineer's assistant, and two electricians. They all promised to return in the morning.

As I examined the break in the film I saw that it had failed at a splice. Since the film was a collection of television commercials glued end to end I decided to take a look at all the other splices. They seemed weak so I respliced all of them.

At about 2:00 A.M. I was checking the 35mm slides when a lamp burned out. But that's easy. The engineer had worried about that and there were plenty of spares. Figuring out how to replace the bulb (or even *find* the bulb) was another matter, but I finally managed.

I then decided that one of the slides was dirty, so I took it out to clean it. I dropped it. (If you're clever, you mount 35mm transparencies between two pieces of glass. That way you keep the film clean. If the glass gets dusty you can very easily wipe off the glass. Also, the focus of the projector is simpler because all the slides ride in the same position when projected.) When I dropped the slide I broke one of the pieces of the cover glass.

This time I didn't bother room service with a request for 2-by-2-inch cover glass. Instead I walked a few blocks across town to our shop and got the material. On the way a hooker asked me if I couldn't think of anything better to do than whatever it was that I was doing. Later on I thought of some remarkably funny things I could have said.

I returned and fixed the slide.

I then noticed that the chairs were arranged funny. So I fooled around with them for a while.

At about 4:00 A.M. I walked uptown and sacked out

at my boss's apartment. He was out of town. I gave some thought to why it was that Good Old Herb was in San Francisco (where it was only 1:00 A.M.) having a good time, while I was in New York having a nervous breakdown over something that seemed so trivial.

I stared at the ceiling and estimated the number of things that could go wrong later that day. I quit when I got up to about fifty-three.

The next morning everybody showed up early for a run-through. We worked out a flashlight signaling system to communicate with the electrician on the dimmers at the other end of the room.

The man who was going to narrate the presentation arrived and was doing fine until I mistakenly showed him the setup in the back of the room. He began waving his arms and saying that it was too complicated— far too complicated.

I felt like screaming, "I agree! I agree!" but instead calmly convinced him that everything would be just fine. We made a successful run-through (during which I noticed that the lectern light would shine in the eyes of the audience, and quickly masked it off).

A few minutes later the audience came in and took their seats. The house lights went down very smoothly, and the lights on the speaker came up full. When he spoke, the volume was at just the right level, with the proper amount of treble and bass. He proceeded easily and introduced the first of the 35mm slides. The lights dimmed on the speaker and the first projector gradually came to its full brightness.

The slide show progressed and, as the last slide dimmed on the screen, the spotlights eased back on the speaker. He then introduced the previous year's film-strip and we cut to a point in the middle of it. This meant turning on the projector, putting the needle down at the right point on the record, and bringing the sound up slowly. It worked. The sequence ended where it was supposed to end. The projector went off and the lights went back up for the speaker to introduce the TV commercials. The film ran through without breaking and the sound level was correct.

At the end of the film, the projector faded to black and the lights went back on the speaker for his brief con-cluding remarks. He finished, the spotlights dimmed, the audience applauded, and the house lights went back up.

Everything had gone smoothly. The audience had been able to hear and see everything with ease. The talk was compact and interesting, enriched with a great deal of visual material.

The audience went back to the buffet and were ready for another easy day.

They left behind a half-dozen people, at least four of whom were drenched with sweat, both from the heat of the equipment and the strain of trying to do things right.

This simple, easy little presentation took just over eighteen minutes, but required about eighteen pieces of gear, several hundred feet of cable, and dozens of man-hours. We spent four hours just breaking things down and putting them back in boxes. It was expensive, in terms of man-hours and equipment rental, but the result was well worth the cost to the client.

From this experience I was able to deduce several things. The first I had already known: audiovisual equipment isn't really portable and shouldn't be moved around very much—it works best if it's installed and left alone. Also, once you get an installation rigged and wired it will be "right" from that point onward with a

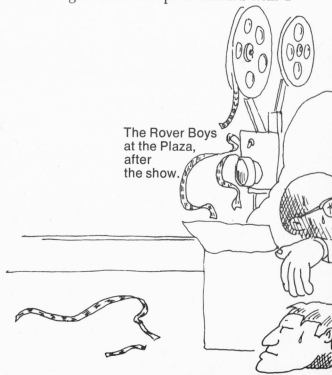

The Rover Boys
at the Plaza,
after
the show.

minimum of maintenance and tweaking of knobs. You should have no further worry about microphones, lenses, or any of the rest of it. In short—make permanent installations.

Another important conclusion was that if you decide to go for broke and do a big, smooth, theatrical number, be sure to allow a little bit of time to do it. Haste makes disasters.

The final conclusion was the simplest. I decided I was too old and nervous for that line of work.

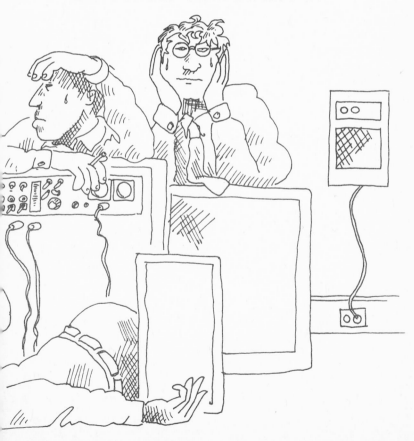

3. Why *I'm* Getting Out of Show Business

I'm sure everyone has heard the story about the guy who smells awful all the time. When asked the reason for this he explains that it's because of his job, working in a circus giving enemas to elephants. The listener asks, "Why don't you get another job?" and the guy replies hotly, "What! And get out of *show business*?"

I was more than ready to get out, particularly if show business meant standing in the back of the Plaza ballroom with my shirt sticking to me. (As things worked out, I needn't have worried. I was caught in an ad agency purge a few weeks later and fired.)

I worked in advertising for a while and then gravitated to the consulting firm of Arthur D. Little, Inc., in Cambridge. My charter was to wander around and try

My performance
was not
flawless in
Washington, D.C.

to help people make better presentations. In the course of doing this without any particular success I was asked by my boss to help with the development of an intensive course called Unified Communications. The subject matter was to include writing, listening, interviewing, group dynamics, reading, and speaking. Would I handle the speaking part and write down everything I knew about presentations?

I said sure I would.

I went home and wrote about half a page.

"Bill," I said the next day, "I have some bad news. Now that I *think* about it, I don't *know* anything about presentations and speaking to groups. I just seem to know when people are doing them wrong."

Bill smiled very slightly and changed the subject to Being Out of Work and Starving to Death.

His observations inspired me to write about twenty pages which, he correctly noted, were devoid of any sense of organization. After several more false starts I developed a series of lectures. The whole idea frightened me pretty badly, simply because it seemed foolhardy to speak to a group on the subject of speaking to groups. Such a presentation must be flawless if the presenter is to be credible.

Flawless it wasn't, and I was incredible. We opened in Washington, D.C., where I speared myself with a pointer, tripped over microphone cables, spilled my notes on the floor, got completely lost a time or two, and screwed up generally.

In the course of doing these lectures elsewhere, I ran into somebody who knew what he was doing. He advised me to let the audience get more involved—give *them* things to do. This, he said, would be good for two reasons. They would have more to keep them occupied, and I wouldn't have to talk so much (thus decreasing the likelihood of my screwing up further).

After that time I began each discussion by dividing the audience into groups of four and asking them what *their* problems were as speakers. They were asked to list their ten most common problems, and, further, to pick a spokesman to come before the audience and discuss them. This technique involved everybody and made speakers out of one fourth of them.

Following these brief presentations, I would ask the same four-man groups to put together a list of the ten most serious problems that an *audience* has. They would then pick a different spokesman to discuss the list.

At the end of the session we would have a great many things to talk about (and by that time, of course, fully half of the class would have participated actively in front of the group).

I have done this now with many groups of people. They have ranged from middle and top management people and business school graduate students to people in typical suburban neighborhoods. The results are always surprisingly the same. Everybody mentions the same things. The average list looks something like this.

People who have to *speak* say:

1. I get stage fright.
2. I have trouble getting, and keeping, attention.
3. I don't have enough self-confidence.
4. I don't know my material well enough to do it easily.
5. I have trouble getting the information together.
6. I don't know what to do with my hands.
7. I have trouble keeping to the allotted time.
8. I don't know how to handle the discussion that *follows* a presentation.
9. I have trouble keeping my *own* interest up.
10. I have trouble organizing information for presentation.

People who have to *listen* say:

1. The speaker was dull, boring, and monotonous.
2. He was very confusing because he wasn't well organized.
3. It was too *long*.
4. The speaker had no convictions about the subject.
5. We couldn't *hear* him.
6. He talked too fast.

7. We were in a bad place. There were too many distractions.
8. The speaker had strange mannerisms.
9. He had no personality.
10. There wasn't anything in it for *me.*

Many other complaints have been made, but these are the common ones, so we'll look at them in greater detail in Chapters 5 and 6, titled "Problems You Say You Have" and "Problems the Audience Says *It* Has Because of You."

If you will *do* something about a few of these simple little items you will succeed. But my experience tells me you won't try. I think it's because you're not really interested.

Let me give you an example. Do you remember the four points I mentioned in the introduction? Do you remember the amount of the reward I'd pay if you ever forgot all four? What western state was I in when my friend told me about the moon? Where did I hear about chewing gum and peanut butter?

Good.

Now, tell me how I ended the introduction. What did I say? I'll give you a clue. I said, "So far in this introduction I've done a few of the key things that a presentation is supposed to do." I listed four key thoughts. What were they?

See? You don't remember.

That's why *I'm* getting out of show business.

Nobody really cares. So I'm going to fold my tent and quit *talking* about presentations, and I'm sure as hell going to quit *doing* them.

This leads me very appropriately to the next chapter.

4. My Advice: Never Speak to Another Audience

The best, most honest, and most heartfelt piece of advice I can give anybody is: *Never speak to another audience again . . . ever!* You will find this the safest, least tiring, and most successful path of all. Quit, because your chances of screwing up are really quite astronomical.

I arrive at this conclusion in two separate ways, one extremely subjective and the other, I think, wholly objective. Subjectively speaking, I have seen great numbers of people attempting to speak in public, but very few who succeeded—very few combined attractive appearance, good speaking voice, ease in front of an audience, and interesting content. I think the reason for this is very simple. The majority of people in our society are very boring. They have little to talk about, and almost nothing to think about. They are the function of many molds and pressures, and they simply don't have anything very distinctive about them. They are Plain Vanilla—at home, at work, at cocktail parties, and certainly in front of groups. It is part of the American upbringing to become self-centered, opinionated, and dogmatic, and these aspects do not play well when one speaks to groups of people.

But, putting that aside, we can find a lot of very compelling *objective* evidence.

I mentioned earlier that an actor or entertainer on a stage has a lot going for him in terms of visual effects, colored lights, nice settings, costumes, makeup, music, careful rehearsals, and so forth.

You have *none* of these things.

It's too bad, because our society has become very sophisticated at *watching* things. People in this country are accustomed to looking at wide-screen movies, color television, plays, nightclub acts, posters, colorful sports, magazines, neon signs, billboards, and all kinds of clever advertising. The most skillful communicators in the world try to get through to us daily.

This represents the competition, and when you stand before a group and serve as the focus of attention you are unconsciously (or consciously) compared with these other media. You come off very poorly by comparison. There is nothing magical about you.

So get out. Don't speak to groups. If you have enough rank in an organization simply announce that as a matter of policy you will no longer make presentations to anybody. About anything.

If you have less rank or status you can say that you read in a respected business review (or *Cosmopolitan*) that people just don't *do* that any more.

Failing that, lie. But take care and always stick to surefire American issues. Say that you will be unable to help with the presentation because you're donating blood for a relative, taking your dog to the vet, visiting a priest, or attending an old person's birthday party.

If none of these works, you may want to get a little more serious about it and try The Mouth Ploy. In this exercise you must avoid talking to people for a few days. If you *must* talk to somebody, cover your mouth with both hands and mumble a lot. Somewhere in the mumbling mention the following two facts: "Dentist said it was a damned close call" and "Gotta go easy on my mouth for a while." This will not only get you out of presentations, but you may actually be shunned by everybody for several weeks.

An alternative to getting out is to find somebody else to make the presentation *for* you. This is really a great idea, particularly if you can find somebody who is good at it, who will devote the time to it, and who will make a point of understanding the information he's supposed to communicate.

The only problem with this idea is that such a person might become little more than a narrator, and wouldn't be able to deal with questions as they came up. But you can handle this somehow. It may be that you can rely on such a person for a formal presentation of facts, leaving you with a less formal, more comfortable question-and-answer period or discussion in a more relaxed atmosphere.

Chances are, though, that you're too unsure of yourself to delegate this responsibility, even though it would limit *your* exposure to the audience to something as safe and simple as, "Thank you all for joining us. I want to begin by reviewing all the aspects of the current problem. I've asked Ed Nordness to handle this end of it, and he's done a comprehensive job. Eddie?"

(It's too bad that serious consideration can't be given to this suggestion. Hundreds of thousands of people in this country have been *trained* to speak other people's words believably. Every year, hundreds of men and women graduate from universities with degrees in theater, speech, and radio/television broadcasting. Only a microscopic part of 1 percent ever make it to Broadway or Los Angeles. The rest are out there percolating through the countryside, selling insurance or encyclopedias, and just waiting for a company or an organization to run an ad reading: "WANTED—*Retread actor or announcer to talk with his mouth for pay. Must look O.K., sound convincing, and know what to do with his hands. No other experience required.*")

But no, you won't try that. Too radical an idea.

But here's something even *more* outrageous! Since I'm sure you won't try to avoid presentations, or relegate the responsibility *for* them, I'm going to suggest you find a *critic*.

I want you to walk up to a subordinate or an associate and say the following:

"Look, Gene, I want you to do something. I'm making a presentation today and I want you to watch it and then talk to me about it afterward. I want you to be honest with me and tell me if I'm doing anything wrong. If I'm picking my nose, or not talking loud enough, or not making any sense, I want you to tell me about it. I want you to see if my facts are clear, or if I even *say* anything. And don't pull any punches. Will you do that, Gene? And not just come up to me later and say, 'Terrific job!'?"

I don't think you will invite anybody to do that. You won't do it because you might get your feelings hurt.

The people who need this kind of help the most are the least likely to ask for it.

They include a wide range of fairly competent (but boring) experts, pompous bureaucrats, and most members of minority pressure groups.

People such as these invariably think that the merit of their ideas, the righteousness of their cause, or the justice of their position will carry the day—and certainly more than offset any defects in presentation.

Well, this is nonsense.

The way information is packaged and delivered is of paramount importance. It is particularly essential for pressure groups of one kind or another to find spokesmen who are articulate, who project well as people, and who can put an audience at ease. Once these qualifications are met, there can be some concentration on the message.

This country has never paid much attention to wild-eyed, incoherent loudmouths. We have vested the real power in people who appear (in public at least) to be calm, considerate, and thoughtful people. They look good. They're even-tempered, yet forceful. They project the feeling that they are capable. This may be the first step in getting elected, or appointed to a position of responsibility.

5. If You *Won't* Quit, at Least Go Someplace Else, or Do Something Different

I've seen a lot of grim conference rooms in this country. And a lot of dismal meeting places. A good many of them have no windows. Most of them are lit with fluorescent lights.

Cool white fluorescent light represents one of the great backward leaps of civilization (second only to office copiers, which put everybody in the publishing business and contribute to the wide-scale proliferation and circulation of garbage). People look like hell under cool white fluorescent lights. They seem too blue and too harsh.

And that's only the light. Most offices and meeting places in schools, businesses, and government facilities are dull, sterile, and deadly. "Office" furniture usually

41

Gray
is not a good color
in an
office.

means awful furniture. Battleship gray still hangs on in a lot of places and, while it may not look too bad on a battleship or an aircraft carrier, it's the most dismal color anybody could pick for a desk, a file cabinet, or the tile on a floor.

Meetings are usually held in the worst places imaginable—in gray little rooms, in funny little auditoriums with fixed seating, or in "conference" rooms containing too much dark wood paneling and enormous tables that serve more to isolate people than to facilitate easy communication. I will complain more about this in Chapter 12, "The Place."

Try not to get stuck with things like that. If you're really determined to talk to a group of people, find an unusual, but suitable, place to do it. Use your imagination.

In the meantime, let me remind you of something you already know about. When did you last have a business lunch with somebody? Or *any* kind of a lunch? Within the last week? Within the last month?

What do you remember about that meeting? Who was trying to do what to whom? Were you trying to persuade somebody to do something? Were they trying to persuade you?

Did anybody succeed?

Chances are pretty good that some business got done, ideas got exchanged, or something pleasant happened.

Restaurants are marvelous places to make little presentations and make other people feel comfortable.

If you take somebody to a restaurant, some benefits automatically accrue to you. Going to a restaurant is something you have to arrange for (and therefore think about) ahead of time. If you have picked a good restaurant the stage setting will be good. You will find plenty of props to work with (knives, forks, salt and pepper shakers, swizzle sticks, and so forth). Chances are you will have good lighting. People look terrific in a good restaurant because a lot of care has been taken with the lights. Women already know a lot of things about this. They know they look like hell if they have to sit in a pool of green or blue light. (These colors don't do a whole lot for food either, except make it look as if it's been sitting outdoors for a long time.) Finally, the "audience" knows he's going to benefit from the lunch, if not from some business, social, or political standpoint, then at least from getting a drink and something good to eat.

His level of expectation going into a restaurant is altogether different from what it is when you lead him into a stinky gym full of metal folding chairs.

You can more easily make somebody comfortable in a good restaurant. And once he's comfortable he is much more disposed to listen to what you have to say.

(This theory holds true for the greatest number of personal relationships. Not too many interesting propositions are developed, or accepted, under cool white fluorescent lights.)

The only problem with a restaurant is that you can talk to only a limited number of people. Any more than six at a table makes successful communication difficult. (Much can be said for keeping groups as small as possible. The more people in a meeting, the greater the chance of confusion and misunderstanding—or, worse yet, anger, fear, and other bad things.)

When you *do* have more people, you've simply got to go someplace else, or do something different. Following are a few ideas.

Private dining rooms in restaurants or private clubs are great, particularly if you can depend on quality service. This is also true of suites in good hotels. You can deal with a larger number of people (such as eight to twelve) with ease. You can have blackboards or easels on hand and create informal, shirtsleeves-atmosphere presentations. You can open a small bar when you feel like it, and serve hors d'oeuvres or a meal.

I've been to meetings in penthouses and they were sensational. So are meetings aboard ships or boats. (They don't even have to *go* anyplace, but can remain tied to a pier.) Trains would be fun, and I've heard of meetings on buses and planes. Lodges, resorts, and motels are naturals, of course.

You can also throw a picnic or relate the meeting to some time-honored activity such as fishing, hunting, or gambling.

I've always wanted to reserve the Goodyear blimp

The Goodyear blimp
would be
a swell place for
a meeting.

for a small meeting some time in Los Angeles. Borrow a couple of stewardesses to serve, and fly low along the California coastline. People would remember that meeting for a hundred years.

Give it some thought.

6. Problems You Say *You* Have

Let's begin with a discussion of some of the problems *you* think you have. I keep hearing things like:

1. I get stage fright.

Well, so do I. Everybody gets stage fright to some extent. A few people only get nervous. Others get physically sick. One of the first things to remember is to shut up about it. Most of the time nervousness doesn't show a bit, and if you keep quiet about it nobody will know the difference. If you mention the fact (or apologize for any other shortcoming in delivery or content) you make the audience very sensitive to it. As they become sensitive to it, *they* get nervous and can't concentrate. They are distracted and can't hear the information you really want them to hear.

Stage fright is a combination of a lot of things, but mainly a function of (*a*) the place, (*b*) the audience, and (*c*) your own material.

You can do something about the first by becoming familiar with the place in which you will give the presentation. If you will be speaking from a stage, you've got to get on it ahead of time. Walk around on it, find the lectern, see where the microphone cables are located and where you operate any necessary projector controls. Find out how to enter and exit comfortably. If there are stairs down to the audience area, walk down them. Walk into the audience area and sit down in a few different seats. Try to understand the view the audience will have of you. Wander around the place for a few minutes. Get familiar with it.

Many readers will now whine, "There isn't *time* to do that. Sometimes I don't even *know* where the meeting is going to be. They sometimes don't decide until the last minute."

You are merely covering up for laziness.

Simply tell people that unless you are told well ahead of time what the facilities are going to be like (and given ample opportunity to inspect them) that you won't cooperate. The deal's off. But *you* have to make a point of it. Nobody else will.

If you must persist in appearing before audiences, you can also do other things to eliminate stage fright. Get plenty of experience, anyplace you can get it. Speak to service organizations. Teach a Sunday School class. Take an evening class in public speaking, or try out for a play. A smart thing would be teaching a class within your own organization, one that meets one evening a week for a few weeks.

A second major cause of stage fright is, of course, the audience. It seems to me that the more you know about them, the easier it is to appear. (Although I know some speakers who find it almost impossible to stand up in front of people they've known for years.)

By and large, however, meeting some of the audience ahead of time will help. Failing that, you can certainly discharge some of your responsibility to acquaint the audience ahead of time with who *you* are, what you're trying to do, what they're expected to do, and how long they're expected to sit there. I'll talk more about that later.

Finally, your own material may be giving you the willies. If you're really not sure of your facts, or the order in which the facts will be presented, you have every right to be terrified.

2. *I have trouble getting, and keeping, attention.*

The answer to this is fairly simple. If you're talking

to the same audiences over and over again, you've probably set a bad pattern. People have a low level of expectation about you that is usually fulfilled.

Your trouble is that you give rotten presentations. They are probably confusing and overly long. Keeping the attention of an audience depends on a whole lot of things, many of which are listed at the end of this book.

You really need the person I told you about—somebody to tell you quite honestly what he thinks. I've developed a special form to help him do that. It is also at the end of the book.

3. *I don't have enough self-confidence.*

Don't worry about it right now.

4. *I don't know my material well enough to do it easily.*

Learn it. I don't like to be abrupt with you, folks, but there are some things you simply can't fake. Obviously, this piece of advice isn't meant to suggest that you learn everything in the world about your subject. You can't do that. There isn't time. Also, there wouldn't be time for you to play it all back to an audience. Know the material *you have chosen* for an audience—the facts you've decided are relevant.

5. *I have trouble getting my information together.*

I know that. It's a real problem. But you know what?

The real issue is that we usually get too *much* information together and don't know what to do with it. We don't know which parts to present and which to set aside. We also get very introspective and forget what the audience *wants* to know or *needs* to know. I think you will be helped with this problem when we talk about audiences.

6. *I don't know what to do with my hands.*

Well, what have you ever *tried* to do with your hands? Anything? You don't just all of a sudden start knowing what to do with your hands. They're a real problem. Here are a few ideas.

If you're really a hopeless case, carry a small stack of 3-by-5- or 5-by-8-inch cards in one hand and carry them at your side at about your waistline. That hand will then be safe and you won't have to worry about it.

Now for the other hand. Put a pencil in it. You can then wave the pencil around a little bit (or, once in a while, hold up the cards and appear to mark them with the pencil—thus making you look very thorough). You can also hold a pipe or a pair of glasses in your right hand. For *rapt* attention, you might try holding a hand grenade, or a revolver in one of the larger calibers.

To really solve the problem you must *exercise,* and do stuff with your hands that you don't normally do. You've got to stop making those halfhearted little gestures in which the hands always hover in an area somewhere between the hips and the belly button.

Get those babies up in the air! Shoot them straight out from the shoulder, first to the left and then to the right. Point your index finger straight out in front of you. Stick both arms up in the air in a big V. Every time you get near a mirror, point at yourself (with a gesture that's kept above the sternum) and shout, *"Hey,* baby!" or "Thattaway to go!" This may startle a few people in the rest room, but don't worry about it.

For another good exercise, try imitating trapeze artists as they give their bows at the end of their act. That's a position in which both arms are fully extended, slightly above the shoulders, with the arms slightly bent at the elbows and the hands outstretched. Chest well out. You can then slowly turn from the left to the right, as though to a whole big circus tent full of people. It's a little tough to work into a presentation, but it's terrific when you finally do.

You can also do some fake swordwork with a yard-

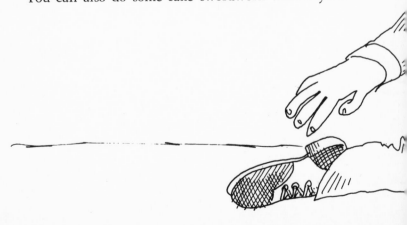

stick, or, almost as good, conduct an orchestra with a ruler. Get in there and put those arms in some positions they don't usually get into. Exercise! *Wave them around!* Pretty soon they'll start doing a few things by themselves.

(I'll tell you what. Put the book down right now, wherever you are. Now make the gesture a baseball umpire makes for *Out!* Or, better yet, the signal for *Safe!* If anybody looks at you strangely, tell them you're in rehearsal for a play about eagles.)

Be a
baseball umpire.
Be an
eagle.

7. I have trouble keeping to the allotted time.

Keep to the allotted time (as defined by you or some-body else), or, better yet, *under* it. Or risk boring every-body to death. It's your choice. Knowing what you're talking about gives you a big advantage in dealing with the problem. One of the greatest rewards you can get from an audience is their gratitude (via smiles, applause, and congratulations) when you successfully reduce one of your traditional fifty-minute ramblings to a tight and lucid ten-minute explanation.

8. I don't know how to handle the discussion that follows a presentation.

Several things must happen in order to solve this problem to the satisfaction of the audience. You have to establish two-way communication; pave the way for some action to take place; invite (and get) participation; and, finally, you must be responsible for the eventual outcome of the things jointly discussed. It isn't reason-able for you to ask for good ideas, get them, and then promptly ignore them. Ideas must be accepted or re-jected, for adequate and understandable reasons.

One technique that works is getting statements or questions from the audience and writing them on a blackboard, or on large sheets of paper that can then be hung up around the room. The audience then sees their own input, and can begin to discuss ways of dealing with it.

If the input is great, chances are it can't be sufficiently discussed in one meeting, and another should be scheduled. You may need to ask for volunteers to follow through, or to make some assignments to specific individuals so that action will result, and progress can be measured.

9. *I have trouble keeping my own interest up.*

That's bad, because an audience can tell very easily if you have any real enthusiasm or excitement for your subject. If you're really not interested in what you're talking about, do as I'm doing. Get out of show business. Learn how to play the violin. Join VISTA. Leave the country. But do something else. Don't inflict your indifference on other people.

10. *I have trouble organizing information.*

This is related to *collecting* information for presentation, and we'll talk about both of them a little later.

7. Problems
   the Audience Says
   It Has
   Because of You

1. The speaker was dull, boring, and monotonous.

I mentioned before that I thought this applied to almost *all* speakers, because of who we are and the mythology we grew up on. "Winging it" is a widespread American tendency. Taking the easy way out is a lot more fun than thinking anything through. Additionally, speakers tend to be dull in direct proportion to their dull surroundings.

2. The speaker was very confusing because he wasn't well organized.

This is also part of being dull and boring. Monotony is generated by people who undertake to tell *everything* they know about a subject. Organization takes some work and a real willingness to communicate useful information.

(I suppose that it's actually a good thing that people are as disorganized as they are. If everybody started communicating in a lucid, forthright way the country would probably collapse. At least 68 percent of the work force would be recognized as superfluous.)

I wonder what really *would* happen if we started to communicate with each other with the same precision, clarity, and simplicity we use to communicate with a computer. A computer isn't very bright; it's merely very fast. Putting anything *in* a computer is a laborious, time-consuming, and very specialized process. A computer is fed little bits of information at a time, in a logical sequence. It isn't given a lot of irrelevant information. Also, you can't kid it along, you don't lie to it, and you can't influence it with emotion. Neither can you threaten it, fire it, or flatter it. The first time you try to cross a computer, it'll get you. Garbage in—garbage out. We can't apply this lesson in human relations, I suppose, because it's not part of the American heritage to show the same consideration for people that we show for machines.

3. *It was too long.*

Same problem as above, with possibly an even greater indifference to the audience.

4. *The speaker had no convictions about the subject.*

We've covered this subject adequately by suggesting that if *you* can't show any enthusiasm, then you can hardly expect such a reaction from an audience. Lack of conviction might be offset by extreme brevity. Speak quickly and sit down.

5. *We couldn't hear him.*

Among the simplest and most rudimentary standards to be met is the demand that the audience be able to *hear* the speaker and to *see* him. Incredibly enough, these obvious rules are broken daily. It is unprofessional, unbusinesslike, and totally unbelievable. Often it's a bureaucratic problem in which somebody of far greater rank is making an ass of himself, but nobody has the nerve to say anything. Buy him a copy of this book and mark this paragraph in red. He will be pleased, not annoyed. Or maybe annoyed enough to change.

6. *He talked too fast.*

Slow down, even though you think it's killing you. You can cure this problem *only* with the help of somebody else—somebody who will listen to you and make an honest report on all the things you're doing. Read aloud slowly. Read against a clock. Read two minutes' worth, and then try to read the passage aloud again in two and a half minutes.

7. *We were in the wrong place. Too many distractions.*

An all too common occurrence, this has happened to everybody—being in a room that was too small, too noisy, too cold, too hot, too stuffy, or had a large picture window overlooking something very interesting.

8. *The speaker had strange mannerisms.*

Women have fewer problems in this connection than men do. Men, for example, have trouser pockets. Men are also more apt to unconsciously scratch some place that itches. I have seldom seen a woman pick her nose. This sort of thing, folks, can become a distraction so great that nobody will hear a word you say.

9. *He had no personality.*

Everybody has a personality. It's simply that most speakers make the worst of theirs. (I don't know if you were aware of this, but personalities can be *changed*. You don't have to stay a dud if you don't want to. For exciting details, send your check for $10,000 to the following address. . . .)

10. *There wasn't anything in it for me.*

There's an entire chapter in this book about the consideration you should give an audience. It's the *next* chapter.

Isn't that convenient?

8. What About the Audience?

The man best qualified (in terms of subject knowledge) to make a presentation is often the worst man to *do* it. He knows too much. The subject has become too much a part of him. He is more apt to think of the subject in terms of its own inherent value, rather than its relationship to other facts, systems, organizations, or to people generally.

He seldom deals with the question that every member of the audience asks: "What's in this for *me* . . . how do *I* benefit?"

They *expect* something.

Remember that your audience looks at you differently from the way they watch television or movies. In the latter case they anticipate pleasure. They hope to be entertained and they are willing to invest time (and money) in this anticipation. They hope for the best, seldom get it, and are not actively critical of what goes on.

People seldom anticipate pleasure, however, when they file into a conference room, meeting hall, or auditorium—and they are quite ready to be critical. They steel themselves for the experience. They are prepared to be confused and numbed by boredom. They know

Some of
the great all-time
surefire persuaders.

well ahead of time that meetings are a pain in the ass.

Later I will give you an idea about how to condition the audience *ahead* of the presentation (Chapter 13, "Prior To"), but right now let's take a look at the audience and some of its real needs and expectations.

Why don't *you* sit in the audience for a minute.

Now then, how can I get you to understand something?

(I am forced, of course, to rule out the six great all-time, surefire persuaders: the promise of food, sex, or wealth; and the threat of death, high levels of pain, or imprisonment. I do this with great reluctance because

even a cursory glance at history shows their widespread use and great effectiveness.)

If I must rely on facts to change your mind, then here are a few of the things you might expect—or at least hope—that I would consider.

1. How much do you, and other members of the audience, already know about the subject?

2. How readily will you understand any specialized language (such as technical terms)?

3. How long have you had an interest in, or a connection with, the subject?

4. How concerned are you with the subject and its ramifications? (Unless I do a little investigating I may gloss over a fact that is of paramount importance to you and the other members of the audience.)

5. How *opinionated* (as contrasted to informed) are you about the subject to be discussed? (I may also try to gauge your opinion about *me,* the speaker, so that I will know ahead of time whether you will be apt to greet me with warmth, indifference, or out-and-out hostility. That kind of estimate should have a profound effect on both the subject matter and the manner of its delivery.)

6. How much help do you need to see the connection

between what I'm *saying* and what you're *doing* (or living, thinking, or understanding)? The essential connection is often overlooked altogether.

7. Why did you attend? This is important to know. Often you attend because you have to, sometimes because you want to. If possible, it's important for me to precondition you to want to be there in the first place.

8. What's in it for *you?* I have to look very carefully to exploit the actual advantages that are going to accrue to you personally—the *benefits* of your listening to me and later behaving in some slightly (or markedly) different way. I must also be alert to the *disadvantages* that may be inherent in my presentation. (What positive, *fun* things can I stress while telling you that the new dam is going to put your town under fifty-seven feet of water?)

If I'm a really clever speaker I will scrounge around to find some special relationship that exists between you and me, or between my organization (or company, church, civic or social group, or political party) and yours. And also find out about the length of that relationship.

I should also investigate all the past attempts at communicating with you, and try to discover the ones that were most successful. (For example, I might discover that you would be more receptive to a presentation that is informal and conversational, instead of one that is serious and highly technical.)

I should try to determine whether there is anything special about the situation (either for me or for you), such as the size of the audience, the time of day (or year), or the special nature of the occasion.

I should give thought to the words I will use, and take a position about *taboo* words.

What is one of the leading taboo words in the English language?

That's correct. Thank you.

One must be very careful in his choice of whether to use "obscene" language. In many cases you will find this not only acceptable and very useful, but desirable. (It is actually a further extension of one's ability to speak conversationally. Swearing is *very* conversational. It is also rich with subtlety and meaning. The old injunction against swearing as a "reflection of one's lack of vocabulary and imagination" is nonsense. If people feel comfortable with it, do it.)

I used to know somebody who would bring a very prim and proper secretary to all his meetings to insure that nobody would use strong language (and therefore say precisely what was on his mind). It forced us into lukewarm questions like, "Golly, we'd sure like to know what the heck's going on down there in the Southwestern Region," when something a whole lot stronger was clearly called for.

(A word about women and swearing. It's still not too easy for women to swear, especially in presentations. It comes as too much of a shock to the male chauvinist pigs and tends to subtract, therefore, from content. Another strategy for women is to refrain absolutely from swearing in a presentation, or even in a conversation, but swear volently when alone [but certain of being "accidentally" overheard]. This should confer quite a bit of mystique—but only if the swearing is done properly. The effect is lost by using foul language unprofessionally, as in "My good hell" or "Hell almighty," or becoming so angry that serious problems of content develop—such as happened when somebody screamed at me, "If you don't like my face, you can *screw* it! And I'm just the guy who can do it!")

So much for language.

A final problem for me to deal with is my *identity*. When a stranger is suddenly presented to you it's only natural to wonder, Who is he? Why is he here? Where did he come from? What can he tell us that we don't know already? This particular identity crisis should be taken care of early.

And I should consider *all* of the foregoing before I decide on the first two words of the presentation.

You may now come back from the audience. It's time to get your stuff together.

9. Getting Your Stuff Together

A lot of interesting material has been written about how to determine the content of a presentation, conduct research for the material, and organize the information. I haven't anything original to add to it, but I've put together another checklist to help you identify some of the loose ends.

Ask these standard, elementary questions when you begin to consider *any* kind of a story.

Who?

Who got us into this? Who warned us? Who lied to us? Who is a part of the problem? (We? They?) Who is in the cast of important characters? Whom can

71

we turn to for help? Who has further information? Who is in charge? Who should be hired? Who should be consulted? Whom shall we assign to work on this? Who is responsible? Who cares? Who has enough enthusiasm to do anything with this?

What?

What happened? In what sequence did it happen? What is *about* to happen? What are the conditions now? What were the conditions that led up to now? What are the events? What was the rationale? What was the plan? What are we going to do? What was the impact of the decision we made last year? What will be the outcome of our actions today? What in the hell is going on?

Why?

Why did this happen? Why did this happen *now* (rather than sooner or later)? Why did this happen in exactly the *way* it happened? Why do we make the decisions we make? Why *us*? Why not *them*? Why did we do what we did? Why didn't we start doing it sooner? Why did we stop? Why don't we get organized? Why are we here?

Where?

Is this going on all over? Or just in Minneapolis? Where did it happen first? Where will it happen next? Where should *we* go? Where should we have gone last year? Where does it hurt us the most? Where can we get some relief? Where does it seem to be working? Where can we get some more of this good stuff?

When?

When did it happen? What time was it? What was the date? Is it continuing to happen *now*? If we'd been clever, when could we have seen this thing coming? When could we have done something? When ·did we really find out? When did we first suspect? When did we begin to react? When are we going to get started on *this* problem? When can we expect to see some progress? When are we going to make some assignments?

And be sure to add one other word to this list:

How?

How *much*? How *often*? How can we react? How can we get there from here? How can we prevent a recurrence? How can we get a piece of the market? How do we proceed?

You must ask (and answer) these kinds of questions in terms of what the audience needs and can understand. This process usually has great value in limiting the kinds of material in a presentation—and the amount of time spent explaining it.

Suppose you were going to tell the story of *Goldilocks and the Three Bears* to an audience who had never heard it. You're unsure of the information. Go back and test the foregoing questions against *Goldilocks*.

In most cases you either know (or think you know) the basic subject matter for a presentation, and you know where additional information can be found. (The problem is not usually the availability or scarcity of information, but knowing how to deal with an *overabundance* of it, and trying to verify its accuracy.)

One well-known and very useful technique for organizing information is to reveal *all* of your key ideas so that you can see them simultaneously.

To do this you put all your key ideas (who, what, where, how much, etc.) on note cards or scraps of paper and spread them out. Be sure to include any thoughts you have about pictures or diagrams that would simplify the story. Once you can see everything—with all the cards in front of you—you can begin to order ideas in sensible ways. It is very tough to organize your material when it's in the form of a stack of papers. You can only see the top sheet of a stack.

A bulletin board comes in handy with the cards. They can be thumbtacked to the board and easily moved from one place to another. As an alternative you can put the pieces of paper on a table or on the floor. The main thing is to be able to stand back a few feet and get a good overall view of the various ideas you hope to present (your content), their relationship to each other (continuity), and the probable speed at which you will deliver them (pace).

The other constant in the equation is the overall time you will spend in the presentation. I wish you would try to keep it short—twenty or thirty minutes.

As you work with this system of spreading things out, you will begin to see new relationships that exist in your material. And, after a while, a natural organization will usually emerge—one that has a logical beginning, middle, and end.

Should this *fail* to happen, and you're left with a collection of unrelated facts, you may have to impose some system that will do the job *for* you.

One obvious system is a strictly *chronological* progression of events in which you say, "Number one happened first, number two happened second, number three, etc." Or you can choose a simple *cause-and-effect* presentation: "The event I'm going to tell you about took place and had an effect on the following five things." Or you might choose a *problem–solution* approach in which you present the basic problem, several possible solutions, and your final choice among those available.

When you are trying to explain a complicated issue or problem, begin by describing the *symptoms*—the effects it is having on people or events. Speakers usually talk about problems in an abstract way, with nothing particularly vital, personal, or immediate about them. But if you can show the impact of the problem on *people,* particularly the audience, you will provoke interest and attention in a hurry.

I can't tell you much more about it because I don't *know* much more about it. You're going to have to sweat it out. There's no magical solution.

I'll say this, though. *Use short words and short sentences.* Simplify the hell out of everything. And figure out the main ideas you really want to leave with people. I've heard teachers say that they're lucky to handle five points in an hour. So that cuts *you* down to a couple.

I'm hoping to get *one* idea across in this book: I want you to show more concern for your audience. I don't really expect you to *grasp* much more than that, and for that reason I've systematized all the detailed information on checklists in the back of the book. You can then make copies of the checklists and carry them with you always (or loan them to somebody you assign to worry about them), and perhaps do a better job next time.

This may be *my* last Last Stand, but it's not yours.

10. Visual Materials That Might Help Your Stuff

There are a lot of ideas about the use of, and need for, visuals, and many of them are good. The main job that visuals are supposed to do is promoting understanding. That's all—just making things easier for an audience to understand.

If I could give you only one rule to remember, it might be this one: "Use a simple visual to express a single idea."

Most people won't do that. They clutter up their visuals with too much miscellaneous material. Visuals such as these simply masquerade as a well-prepared outline or careful work. In this case, everything the *speaker* needs to know is abridged on to one or two slides, and he can then talk for an hour and fifteen minutes. During this time the slide may (or may not) be explained to those members of the audience who are still awake.

The problem is not wholly the speaker's. Merely a slob trying to survive, he will try anything. He was told, after all, that it was *easy*.

They told him. And let me now direct a few kind

words to *them,* the folks who brought us the Audio-visual Revolution.

Equipment manufacturers have done a slick job of selling audiovisual equipment to just about everybody in the country. And the largest portion of this equipment is sitting in storerooms gathering dust, because nobody knows how to use it. It was advertised to look so easy that *anybody* could do it. And it's quite true that just about anybody can turn the equipment on and off or lug it around. But very few people know how to *design* audiovisual material. Fewer still know how to produce the material once it's designed. And then we

**A-V equipment manufacturers
have done
a great selling job.**

reach the real minority—those who know how to *use* the material effectively once it's produced.

It is a miserable bitch of a job and requires a high level of imagination, creative ability, experience, and skill. It also takes unusual care and a considerable amount of time. So I'm sick of the abundance of literature that explains how simple and easy everything is.

As if the audiovisual "revolution" weren't enough of a hoax, we are now being set up for another sucker play in the form of a Video Casette Revolution in Business and Industry. I suspect this new equipment will first be sold to just those places already loaded up with dusty audiovisual equipment. The same people who were deluded in the first place will now be persuaded to "upgrade" their facilities and capabilities with video tape.

Once again, the whole thing will look so effortless. *Anybody* will be able to produce TV on his first attempt. No training, planning, or thinking needed.

It is truly wonderful.

Let us advance to something much easier to understand.

Blackboards

I had intended to say that blackboards represent the one thing that Audiovisual Experts haven't been able to screw up. But this isn't true. The other day I tried to use a *white* blackboard. It was designed for use with greasy crayons. A marvelous idea—flawed only slightly by the fact that it doesn't work worth a damn. You can't see most of the colors, and you can't get the colors off the board once you get them on. A real disaster.

(I was chided recently by somebody who said that I should always say *chalk*board, since blackboards are seldom black any more, but are frequently green or some other color. I told him that I would continue calling them *black*boards in the hope they would all be made that way again. Blackboards provide greater contrast.)

Anyway, a blackboard is a nice, cheap, big, simple, easy thing to use. It hasn't got a cord to trip over, and there's nothing in it that can burn out suddenly. You can put a great deal of trust in your average blackboard. (It is *possible,* I find, to tip one over, but it takes a great deal of doing.)

The blackboard is not only a handy visual device, it is also a giant prop. It provides you with a place to go (such as away from the lectern), and it gives you something to do with your hands. You can walk up to it, write something on it (or erase something from it), and walk away from it. This movement might provide the only variety in an otherwise boring and static presentation of facts.

A blackboard has a number of other advantages. You can make changes easily, there is plenty of room, and you create the illusion that the information you put on it is very current—that the data are being revealed for the first time.

Another benefit, of course, is that you can display

some of your audience's thoughts on it, thereby getting more involvement and commitment on their part. People in the audience *love* to look at their ideas written in big letters for all to see.

The best blackboard system has several boards mounted on tracks so they can roll back and forth in front of each other. Such a system enables you to prepare complex drawings or sets of figures ahead of time, and roll them into view when needed.

Charts

There are two kinds of charts you may be familiar with—the stiff kind made from illustration board (these are almost impossible to carry around, particularly on airplanes), and the flexible paper kind that can be rolled up. The latter are also called "flip" charts because the individual sheets flip over the top like pages in a book.

Some fairly small flip charts are intended for conference room or office situations where they can be used on a table top with small audiences. Whatever their size, charts of this type are made up in advance. (I'm not going to try to tell you how to make professional-looking charts because we'd be here all night, and also because I don't particularly believe in them. If you must use charts of this sort, get somebody who knows what he's doing and pay him whatever you have to in order to get a good job.)

I believe in easel pads. An easel pad is merely a large pad of newsprint paper mounted in such a way that the individual sheets can be torn off or flipped over the top of the pad. The pad is mounted on a large tripod-type holder about six feet high. Easel pads can be marked on with grease pencils or with fat, juicy, felt-tip markers.

Easel pads are cheap and easy to write on. You can produce great lists of ideas and problems and then tape these lists all over the walls of a room. Such a display of thoughts (easily added to or subtracted from) greatly aids in problem-solving. Important relationships between the information on the east wall and the data on the north can suddenly emerge.

The thing I like the most about both easel pads and blackboards is that the speaker himself generates the visual materials. This process keeps him active, mobile, and animated, and lends a sense of immediacy and spontaneity to the information being presented.

All that is required of the speaker is legible handwriting—in letters large enough to be seen by the people in the back of the room. His lettering doesn't need to be artistic, merely visible and understandable.

Projectors

Two types of projectors are sold—one type for showing opaque materials and the other for transparent materials.

An opaque projector is about the size of a small ele-

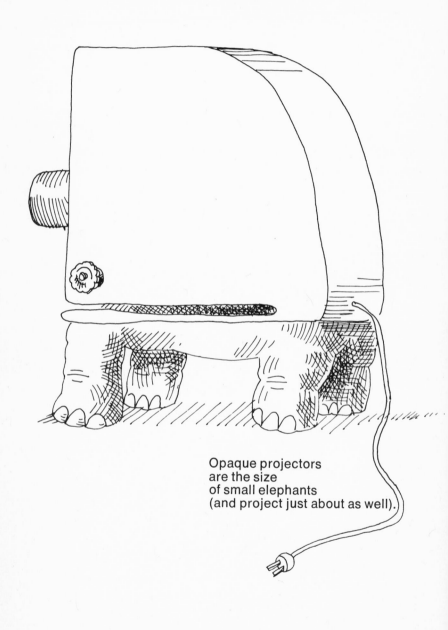

Opaque projectors
are the size
of small elephants
(and project just about as well).

phant and just about as handy. It is designed to project pages from books, pages from reports, and a lot of other things you shouldn't be using anyway. Forget all about it.

You will encounter two basic types of projectors for transparencies: overhead projectors, and slide projectors of various sizes (the most common of which is 35mm).

Overhead projectors use a transparency about 8 by 10 inches in size that lies flat when projected. A light source underneath the transparency shines upward through it. Part of the light is collected in a periscope-like device, the optics of which direct the image onto a screen. The rest of the light goes up to the ceiling, a fact that disturbs me somewhat. Projectors of this sort also make me nervous because people won't go to the trouble of angling the screen to prevent the inevitable distortion (keystoning) of the projected image.

Overhead projectors are easily abused because the large format enables people to put enormous amounts of stuff on them, and then use them as crutches instead of as honest aids to the audience.

Two interesting features are that you can write on them with colored grease pencils, and you can produce overlays that gradually "build up" an explanation of a complicated idea. The two features can be used together by a speaker who wishes to write down a problem, discuss it, and then use an overlay to show the solution more quickly. It would be faster than taking the time to write the solution in your own hand.

There are ways of making an overhead transparency from a typewritten page, but I advise you not to use any of them. I urge you instead to join me in walking out of any presentation that uses a visual produced from a typewritten page. It can't be seen by an audience of more than two people, and *they* have to be seated within three feet of the screen.

With regard to audiovisual products of this kind, it's difficult to decide which is the more preposterous: the absurdity of the idea or the irrationality of the customer who would buy it.

I have nothing to say about the production of overhead transparencies. Plenty of publications have explained how easy they are to produce. Why don't you go try it and then get back to me.

We'll have a couple of laughs.

35mm Slides

These have become the virtual standard for use in presentations. A few people still use lantern slides, which are about 3¼ by 4 inches. They require a projectionist, while most 35mm projectors can be operated by the speaker himself using a remote advance-retreat control.

I have very little to say here about photography, except to describe a paradox. A great many advertising dollars have been spent in this country to persuade people that they can take pictures. And, indeed, they *can*. There are a great many very competent picture-takers in the population. A few of them even go on to become photographers. There are millions of cameras in this country.

But why is it that so few photographs (either prints or slides) are used in presentations?

I'll explain why. The acquisition of a still photograph is a fairly straightforward proposition—a consideration of films, lenses, meter readings, and composition. The problem arises in the selection and organization of a *series* of pictures that are to be used to tell a *story*.

Here we bog down—not merely in pictures, but in words. It is a very complicated business that requires more care than we're usually willing to take, or more imagination than we've got. The production of an audio-visual presentation requires more than the services of a photographer or a writer. It requires somebody who can think in terms of both verbal and visual images. Very few people of this sort can be found in business communications; they are more apt to be working in television or film production.

Supposing, for the moment, that you *have* some slides, let me pass along a rule that *I* try to use. I don't

like to be in the same room with a projector. Projectors belong in little projection rooms, alcoves, boxes, or someplace other than in the room where I'm trying to talk. They make noise and emit stray light, neither of which I need when I'm trying to control 100 percent of the audience's attention.

It isn't much of a hassle to put a small window in one wall of a room you use for presentations. Even if there's an office on the other side of the wall, a projector operating for a few minutes now and then won't cause any important disruption.

I will conclude this section with three tips about 35mm slide production. Use an incident light meter (and occasionally a tripod) in taking the slides, and a dissolve unit in projecting them. (A dissolve unit is used in conjunction with two projectors to make smooth transitions between slides. As the light of the first projector dims, the light of the second projector—carrying the next slide—brightens proportionally. One picture "dissolves" or overlaps into the next. This avoids the choppy effect of going to black between slides, which is characteristic with one projector.)

Other kinds of projectors include, of course, movie projectors. They *really* should be kept out of the room, because the larger ones are quite noisy.

Room Lights

When you use any kind of projector, you must make provisions to darken the room. The best way to do this is to *dim* the room lights, project the material, and bring the lights back to average brightness.

Nothing is worse than throwing a switch and plunging a room into complete blackness. (Unless it's throwing a switch and turning all the lights back *on*, blinding everybody in the process.) Rheostats don't cost very much, and enable the lights to be dimmed to any comfortable level.

Things to Remember about Visuals

Despite my grumbling, I very much favor using visuals, particularly if they happen to be good and can be used gracefully. Their use must always be made to *seem* easy and simple, despite the fact that they're difficult to produce and use properly. Here are a few hot tips about production.

1. Use the simplest terms and relationships you can possibly think of.

2. Show only highlights.

3. *Never* exceed forty characters (including spaces) across a visual of any kind.

4. Never exceed eight lines.

5. Omit subtitles and other extraneous words; *you're* there to pass along this information.

6. Don't use vertical printing. The audience can't turn a screen on edge as they can a page.

7. Use a minimum number of curves on graphs. Three should be the absolute limit.

8. Use the minimum number of grid lines.

9. Don't use complete sentences—only key words or phrases.

10. Allow one visual to amplify one idea.

That's enough.

Insist on one thing: that the people who design and produce your visuals attend a rehearsal in which their stuff is used. They will learn something from this expanded experience and will be able to detect problems in time to fix them. (A lot of people produce materials that they never see projected on a screen, so they think their responsibility ends at the drawing board. You must try to extend it.)

Books about presentations always contain lots of detail about the visual choices the speaker can make, and provide plenty of information about charts, slides, movies, flannel boards, magnetic boards, models, video tape, filmstrips, and so forth.

Those are the conventional things.

I'm anxious to pioneer some other visual techniques such as indoor neon signs, tattooing, cave painting, theater-in-the-round, pantomime, flags and pennants, needlework, puppets, and mosaic tile.

You're welcome.

11. Some Thoughts About Your Mouth and Using It Up There In Front of People

I keep harping about the need for an objective evaluation of your performance in front of an audience. You *need* this. And somebody (or some group of people) has to do it for you. Some people recommend using a television system in which you rehearse in front of the camera and then watch yourself on a playback monitor. I'd rather you didn't go through this process by yourself (particularly the first time or two). You should have somebody with you who can explain what's happening.

There are quite a number of things to look for in a speaker—so many, in fact, that a checklist is needed to keep track of them. One such checklist can be found at the end of this book. It doesn't offer too much from everybody else's checklist, it's merely named differently.

These are usually called things like Speaker Analysis Form, Peer Evaluation Sheet, or—more pompously—Functional Verbal Appraisal Record.

I call mine a Grunt Detector (Checklist L).

It's divided into several basic parts, covering how you *sound*, how you *look*, and how you've managed *to get your information across*. This chapter limits itself to how you sound and look.

A few items have specifically to do with your *voice*.

Go thee forth and shout soliloquies from *Hamlet*.

Volume

The meaning of the word is easy enough to understand, but just the same a lot of people just won't *speak
up*. Why? Nobody *tells* them they aren't speaking
loudly enough. A speaker *must* be heard by everybody
in the audience. (That's the main reason for being there
in the first place.) He shouldn't have to strain or waste
a lot of extra energy. I've worked with actors and other
people with this problem. I've taken them out into a
field and made them yell. You should try it. You may
get arrested, but what the hell. You'll get some idea of
what you can do. (*Don't* scream as loud as you possibly
can. You might ruin yourself. Just be *loud*. Some of
Hamlet's soliloquies are excellent for shouting. Try it.
Take a couple of cans of beer with you. Better yet, find

somebody else with the same problem, and take *two* copies of *Hamlet,* plus more beer. The two of you can then stand about fifty yards apart and yell Shakespearean stuff at each other. Also, take yardsticks so that while you're yelling you can also do a little swordwork, or otherwise practice some gestures that are as broad as your voice is loud.)

Tone of Voice

In normal conversation you vary the tone of your voice (as well as its volume) quite naturally. Your voice changes to the same degree that your subject matter has variety. You should make an effort to bring this naturalness to the front of an audience. One of the reasons you should never *read* a speech is that there will be insufficient intonation. Unless you're a radio announcer you'll drift into a monotone, with absolutely *no* variety.

Quality of Voice

There are ways of dealing with a voice that is too high or too low, or with the problem of talking through your nose. Speech therapists do that. I can warn you of a common problem, however, that you *can* do something about. *Don't* speak to a group if you are hoarse or your voice is raspy. It drives an audience absolutely wild, and they spend the whole time coughing and hacking trying to clear *your* throat.

Diction

You've got to enunciate. You must not mumble and continually slur words. Many of us don't enunciate as clearly as we might, and it may take a lot of practice to solve the problem. Try speaking very clearly with your teeth clenched. Recite *Mary Had a Little Lamb* with your teeth clenched—and really work those lips!

In the meantime, don't make matters worse. Don't stick a pipe or a cigar in your mouth, and don't chew gum. Also, lay off the sauce prior to a presentation. You may *think* a couple of drinks will help, but they usually don't.

Breathing

This is an automatic process that normally allows us to get through a sentence without running out of breath. We do it quite naturally. There's probably something very wrong with you if you have trouble in normal conversation. *Any* time you read aloud, however, you're apt to get into trouble. In this case it is very easy to run out

of breath unless the material has been written very carefully. So don't read to people. Ever.

(The one time you should read material aloud is
when you're *writing*. This is a free writing tip. The
next time you're working on the draft of a written piece,
take it someplace and read it aloud. If you find it difficult to read out loud, then you can be sure that the
reader will have trouble with it. Short sentences are
both easier to say and easier to read. I learned this the
hard way. In the narration recording session for the first
industrial film I ever wrote, the announcer ran out of
breath for the third time, threw the fifteen-page script
up in the air, and walked out of the studio. The recording engineer called me on the intercom to say, "I
think he had a little trouble reading your script.")

Skill in Phrasing

What does this mean? Simply that you shouldn't
hang your sentences together with a lot of "and's" and
"uh's." You can only get over this habit by thinking
about it. If you sense you have a problem and want to
do something about it, take somebody to lunch and
make him promise to bang his fork on his glass or stick
out his tongue at you every time you put two sentences
together with "and" or "uh." It will probably ruin that
particular relationship, but you might learn something.

(I am personally afflicted with a "you-know" problem and am apt to end most sentences with "You know?" If I had fifty cents for every time I've said that in the last six months I wouldn't have to sit here writing this book. I'd be sitting in a sidewalk cafe on the Riviera.)

General Nervousness

If you get nervous, *never say anything about it*. To anybody. At any time. Chances are they'll never know. We always look far less nervous than we really are. Also, don't jangle keys or change. Don't fidget. Fight to remain calm. Get more familiar with your surroundings. Get more familiar with your audience. Rehearse. And rehearse with people, not by yourself. Rehearse with your spouse, or a close friend. Or both. Round up some neighbors and pay them a dollar. If all else fails, talk to your dog. Chances are he'll stand very patiently and look like he's trying to understand.

Enthusiasm

If you have any interest in the subject at all, you shouldn't have any trouble communicating this interest to an audience. Enthusiasm is contagious. You have to get yourself "up" for a presentation in much the same way an athlete does for a sporting event. You may find it useful to do a few mild calisthenics immediately prior to your appearance before a group—but only enough to wake you up, and not enough to make you short of breath.

Posture

You shouldn't slouch or drape yourself over lecterns and other furniture. Try to get away from lecterns. They place an obstacle between you and the audience. Force yourself to stand up straight—without looking stiff or unnatural. You may feel a little uncomfortable, but I want you to *look* good. Looks may be the only thing going for some of you.

General Appearance

Dress neatly. Comb your hair. Shine your shoes. Clean your nails. Don't chew gum. Don't wear clothes that make people laugh. And don't drink booze because it can make your eyes look weird. (I thought I had some special advice for women, but I see that it applies equally well to men: try to lower your voice a little, don't burst into tears, and don't dress provocatively.)

Facial Expression

In ordinary conversation your facial expression alters right along with changes in volume and tone of voice. It is a function of what you're saying, and you do it naturally. The more conversational you can make your presentation, the less you will have to worry about it. *Don't* try to practice in front of a mirror. You'll only screw yourself up. It's a lot like having your picture taken. You sit there and wonder what to do with your face. (Women have less of a problem with this than men. I believe it's because they use mirrors more often than men do, and have therefore learned some things about themselves.)

Eye Contact

Look at people when you talk to them. That's not asking too much, is it? And shift your gaze and your attention among various people; don't talk only to a select one or two. Whatever you do, don't look at the ceiling. Or the back wall. Or your shoes.

Gestures

In normal conversation with people we don't hesitate to use our hands, our arms, or our entire bodies (such as when we recount a fishing story or a golf story). But some people just can't figure out what to do with themselves in front of an audience. President Nixon is among those thus afflicted (although I'm beginning to see signs of improvement). At one time his arms and hands seemed to be under the control of an unseen puppeteer, or a computer in some faraway place.

Stand up for a minute. Put your hands loosely at your sides. Now put your left hand at your side and your right hand at your waist. Put your hands in back of you, holding your right wrist with your left hand. Fold your hands loosely in front of you. If you have back pockets put your hands in them.

The next time you watch television, pay attention to what people do with their hands. Go see an Italian movie.

Remember something. If you have visuals or props to handle during a presentation, be sure to rehearse with them well ahead of time. It will help you to use them naturally and comfortably.

I talked about gestures earlier. Do you remember exactly where? Can you turn back to it right now?

Stay on your toes!

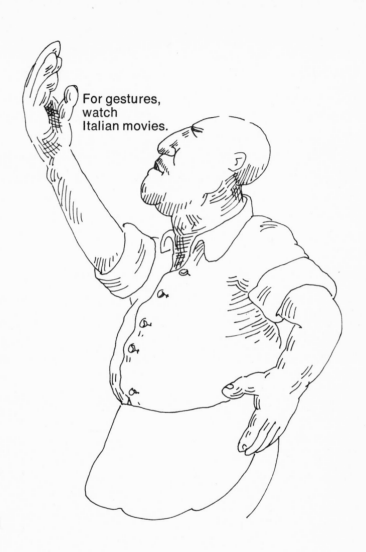

For gestures,
watch
Italian movies.

Rapport

What was the response of your last audience to you?
Was it warm? Was it cool?

You really don't have to *do* very much to get inter-
action with an audience. You only have to treat them
with a little respect.

At one time I worked briefly with a minority group
trying to get a couple of people elected to office. I kept
stressing the need for a candidate who would at least
be neat, clean, prompt, reasonably forceful, and possess
a passing acquaintance with English grammar. But it
never worked out that way.

The guy who showed up on television was inevitably
late, angry, without a jacket, with tie undone, glistening
with sweat, and screaming uncontrollably that he and
the rest of his kind were "being robbed and screwed" by
the system.

What he was saying was true. The system *was* sys-
tematically robbing him and screwing him.

The audience, however, wasn't about to be persuaded. When speaking to robbers and screwers you've
got to be at least as clever as they are, and sensible
enough to employ *their* weapons.

12. The Place

I mentioned this problem in Chapter 5, if you recall.
I haven't changed my mind.

The place in which you choose to communicate
should be a *nice* place. It should be a pleasant and interesting place. It might even be beautiful.

Most people in this country have been taught the
absurd maxims, "You can't judge by appearances" and
"Appearances are deceiving."

Of course you can judge. You do it all the time. Appearances *aren't* deceiving. The appearance of a thing
is an excellent indicator of what the thing really is. We
go through life affected very largely by how things appear, and how they feel, and how they move us. The
word we've created to describe this nonverbal sense of

the rightness or wrongness of things is "vibes"—vibrations. We trust them.

The *place,* therefore, should be chosen from the standpoint of making things look easy, and comfortable, and relaxed. The environment should make the audience *feel* good. They ought to get good vibes, because if they do they'll be more receptive. Tension and strain will be reduced.

If the place appears gloomy and uncomfortable, the audience will be turned off. They will be further turned off if the speaker is flapping around getting things pulled together at the last minute. His scurrying around makes everybody tense (because of him and *for* him). This kind of nervousness spreads easily. You can add to it very easily with confusion about projectors and where to plug them. People can run around looking for light switches. Drapes can be pulled. Screens can be noisily run up and down.

People will sit in their chairs wishing they were someplace else instead of being subjected to something that looks ratlike and frenzied—as though they had been invited to witness an animal squirming in a trap.

A meeting place should be regarded in much the same light as a living room, a clubhouse, or a private room in a good restaurant. The expectation should be created that things are going to come off easily and well, and that everybody will have a pleasant time.

In effective communications, appearances are *vital.*

Let me proceed with some ideas about changing some of the old places you've been using, or in designing new ones.

One of the first things you can do, if you're afflicted with fluorescent lights, is urge people to buy *warm* white fluorescent bulbs. They will make a world of difference and everybody will look a lot better.

In designing an area for meetings and presentations I suggest sticking with incandescent lights. For the sake of flexibility I would put them on a lot of different circuits, and put each circuit on a dimmer. In this way you can selectively light any area you choose.

A few other simple ideas will contribute to an optimum facility:

1. More than one exit

2. Restrooms nearby

3. A suitable (and quiet) air conditioning and ventilation system

4. A small projection room from which projectors shine onto a screen. I don't care much for rear-screen installations, where the people running the equipment can't see the same thing the audience is seeing. In any event, a projection room will insure that the audience won't have to listen to the buzzing and clacking of the projectors. Once

you set up a projection room, by the way, the equipment should not be moved from it. I've told you already that audiovisual equipment isn't really portable. The less you move it, the less chance it will screw up. So keep it in one place. Keep equipment covered when not in use. Clean it regularly. And keep the door locked so people won't walk off with it. Also, use *experts* for projectionists, not just anybody who happens to be standing around in the hallway.

5. Rugs on the floor

6. Table lamps

7. Interesting colors and textures. Don't paint the place gas-chamber green, or use a lot of wild patterns.

8. Variable lighting. Arrange it so you can darken the room. Have window drapes backed with a lightproof material. (On the other hand, make the windows large enough so you can admit plenty of sunlight when it's available.)

9. No phones

10. Sliding corkboard panels that move to one side to reveal a blackboard

11. High enough ceilings

12. Good acoustics

13. Cleanliness and order at all times

14. Comfortable places to sit. Let me speak about this important point at greater length. A lot of mistakes are made in this area: one of the gravest blunders is installing rows of seats that can't be moved. I can understand the need to do this in a movie theater, but most other places should have movable chairs. In a bolted-down row of seats the only people you can talk to (by craning considerably) are those to your immediate left or right. Chairs in a meeting area should be comfortable and movable, and the room should permit a great many chair arrangements—big circles, small circles, horseshoes, and ovals. Any way that meets the exact needs of the group and the subject to be discussed.

15. No tables. Tables inhibit the communication of ideas, and large conference tables actually help to proliferate garbage. I'm sure you've noticed that people bring lots of Xerox copies of things to meetings held around a large table. They know that each person will have a large piece of table in front of him to *store* things—tablets and pencils, notes, reports, and Xerox copies of all the things that other people brought. Soon the place on the table in front of the person becomes more important than the person himself. Nobody pays

any attention to the person's *mind,* or *telling* him things—they merely pass down reams of paper to the person's chunk of table. The person later wanders away with all his paper and a strange mixture of certainty and confusion. He's certain he's not going to read it, but he's uncertain about throwing it away. So it gets filed.

Meetings should be held without anything that can act as camouflage or armor. People should meet once in a while without pencils or paper . . . or even pockets, such as outdoors in swimming suits.

It would improve communications.

13. Prior To

This chapter is divided into three subparts entitled *Well Prior To* (meaning more than a week), *Somewhat Prior To* (meaning two or three days), and *Immediately Prior To* (meaning minutes).

Well Prior To

You can score extra points well before a presentation ever starts. One of the first, and probably the most important, is with *invitations*.

For fast, thrown-together meetings, a phone call will do just fine. You can talk to people and advise them of when, where, and what to expect.

For a more formal kind of presentation, or one in which all or part of the audience is unknown to you, you should send a written notification such as a memo.

A memo can serve a variety of purposes, a couple of which are political, but they mostly do an honest job of telling the audience what to expect.

Such a memo should include the place the presentation will be held, the date and the time, and an agenda of what will be included (with some sense of how long a period of time it will take). The memo can also briefly describe something of the subject matter, and the credentials of the speaker.

Such a memo may also suggest that the audience bring something *to* the meeting, such as past records, notes, or ideas.

Determine well ahead of time whether the meeting will be informal. A formal meeting is one in which you do not expect much in the way of audience participation. You progress through your material without any questions from the audience. If any questions are accepted, they wait until the end. An *informal* presentation invites participation from the audience at any time.

Somewhat Prior To

Get onto the stage or into the front of the presentations area. Walk around the stage and get familiar with it. Handle the microphones. Work with blackboards, easels, and props. Check the lights, and insure that the right kinds of projection equipment will be on hand when needed.

The main thing at this point is to rehearse adequately. Without rehearsal you will find that words don't come out as easily as you expected them to. You fumble. You go into your famous "uh," "ah," and "hmmmm" number.

You try to use the blackboard and the chalk explodes. The easels fall over. You drop things. And trip over cords. And each time these petty annoyances take place you lose more of your train of thought. Finally you lose it altogether and you stop dead. Stunned. Silent.

Rehearse sufficiently and you'll not only get through the presentation successfully, but you'll be able to answer questions more easily. It often happens that rehearsal in front of another person will show up gaps in your information or holes in your logic.

Immediately Prior To

Go someplace and loosen up your voice by singing, shouting, or speaking in an overly loud voice. Go "Mi, mi, mi, mi, " or "Fa, fa, fa, fa," a few times. Get your voice out of your normal conversational register. Also wave your arms around and perhaps jump up and down a few times.

By getting yourself physically "up" for the meeting you also raise your emotional and intellectual levels.

Go to the bathroom. Get a drink of water. Focus your attention on your subject matter and keep it there for a few minutes prior to the presentation. If you're comfortable about everything you'll be able to chat with a few people before the presentation. If you're not quite that comfortable, concentrate up to the last minute.

Then go out there and let them have it.

14. During

The trouble with presentations is that so many things are happening at once. You have to be concerned with your material, yourself, your audience, and the environment (plus all their complex interrelationships). A book can discuss these aspects one at a time, but *you* have to endure them simultaneously (and in an environment that is usually neither friendly nor familiar).

Your material has its own special set of requirements. It has to be unfolded in a certain way to make any sense. And it must keep them interested. While visual materials may aid in the understanding of the information, they also pose problems in setup and handling.

The problems *you* face as an audiovisual aid have been discussed in detail. They include how you look

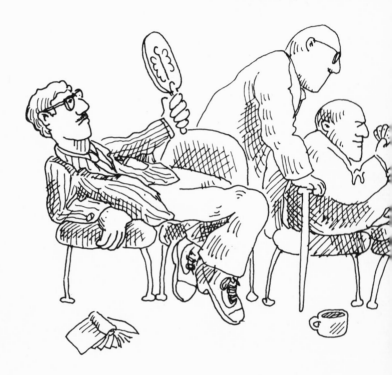

and sound, whether you're interested or not, excited or not, nervous or not.

The audience has *its* worries that must be calculated. They may be tired, hungry, thirsty, bored, angry, or just badly in need of a break.

The environment contributes to audience comfort, but poses a set of potential dangers to you. Equipment fails. Jackhammers start up outside. Things go haywire.

Use the checklists at the end of this book. They will

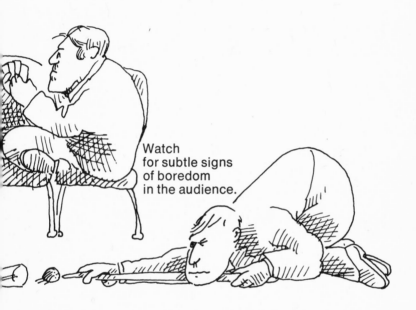

Watch
for subtle signs
of boredom
in the audience.

help to minimize the number of outside things that can go wrong (or simply will never be assured of going right until somebody devotes attention to them). You should improve your next presentation by at least 50 percent by worrying about just a few of the *little* things.

While you're up there in front of everybody juggling all these considerations you must also watch the audience very carefully and try to react to what they're doing (or failing to do).

If you've made an honest effort to get organized and can keep your presentation as short as possible, chances are you won't bore them.

If it looks like you've lost them, you should summarize quickly and sit down.

Keep your eye on people. You have to be completely blind to avoid seeing obvious signs of boredom and nervousness. They include:

1. Not looking at you
2. Cleaning fingernails
3. Doodling
4. Yawning
5. Passing notes and repressing laughter
6. Looking intently at the wall behind you
7. Looking out the window
8. Jerking suddenly upright after having dozed off
9. Reading other material
10. Outright sleeping

A miserable trick to play is identifying somebody who is obviously not paying attention and firing a question at him: "That *is* the right number, isn't it, Ed?"

That may galvanize the audience for just a little while. But not for long.

15. After

After the presentation you may wish to distribute handouts that cover the highlights of your material. You may also want to lead a discussion that can decide on action to take now that you've *made* the presentation. In any event, you must be prepared to answer questions or objections.

Even though these things take place *after* your talk, you should mention them ahead of time. It will make the audience more attentive if they know their participation is expected at the end.

You perform a real service if you indicate to an audience that you will provide handouts of the highlights of your presentation. It relieves them of the need to take notes. You can't expect them to remember large volumes of information anyway.

You should provide handouts for the audience if you have been talking about complex data such as figures, tables, graphs, or drawings. They may consist of some of the actual visuals used (but in a modified form to include titles and legends), or other interpretive or explanatory notes.

The handout should meet these simple tests: Is this important to an understanding of my ideas? Will it help to achieve my objective?

Above all, distribute handouts *after* you've said what you wanted to say, not before. If you distribute a handout before you speak, you invite the audience to read rather than listen to you.

They will also rattle the paper.

Having made the presentation you will also want to deal with the question of *follow-through*, to insure that some appropriate action takes place as a result of your presentation.

This can be a two-part proposition. You can tell the audience, or selected members within that audience, what you expect *them* to do, establishing dates and deadlines by which work or effort is expected. You may also wish to tell the audience what *you* intend to do, and by when. (Living up to that commitment may be the determining factor in the credibility of your presentation—in other words, "He told us what he was going to do, and he *did* it.")

The last of your after-presentation considerations is

your ability to handle the questions or objections that may arise at the end of the presentation.

You should take some special pains to provide whatever backup material you might need to provide proofs, verifications, or explanations.

If you really get pinned to the wall, you may wish to get out of it by using (very firmly) such things as:

1. To be quite frank with you, I don't have that information with me. I'll have to get back to you.
2. Since that information isn't of particular interest to the entire group, we'll discuss it at some point after the meeting.

There are two great all-time stratagems to employ when you're asked a question and need some time to think of an answer.

The first requires a lot of nerve and stage presence. You listen to the question, and then say, "I'll have to think about that for a minute."

Then you stand there and think about it for a minute. It drives an audience up the wall to see somebody that cool.

The other thing to do (and probably better) is to *rephrase the question or the objection.* Very casually say, "Do I understand you to say that you think . . ." and then provide a somewhat longer version of the question or objection.

While you're stalling this way you have a chance to think of an answer. You can also count on gaining time because the original questioner will inevitably want to embellish your embellishment of his original questions. This, of course, gives you a chance to attack his later embellishment instead of dealing with the real issue. (You are bound to find some small error in judgment or logic by comparing his two statements.)

In some cases he will develop his question into a statement, or even a minor address. In either case you're clearly out of trouble.

Like any good salesman, you've got to minimize objections and capitalize on any points on which you and the audience can reach agreement. You've got to get their heads nodding affirmatively and keep them that way.

As I've tried to explain, the process of getting people to nod agreement begins well ahead of the presentation, with an intelligent invitation and an intelligent explanation of what is expected of them. Everything you *do* contributes to ultimate success and is worth the investment of time or expenditure of energy.

16. Much Later

Checklist L in this book is called a Grunt Detector. It can be used by those who review your next appearance in front of an audience.

(I say *those* because it may be easier for you to find a *group* of people to give the forms to, rather than one individual who might feel awkward about it. Give copies to several people and let them return the forms without their names on them. In this way you can average the inputs and perhaps arrive at a more honest appraisal of yourself.)

Within Checklist L are buried the following questions that should be asked after *any* presentation.

1. Did it get off the ground either immediately or eventually?

2. Did it consider mutual interests, aspirations, and points of view?

3. Did it use understandable language?

4. Did it *say* anything?

5. Was it worth the *time*?

6. Was it thoughtfully prepared (to the point where there could be no misunderstanding)?

7. Did it begin to open two-way communication or stimulate discussion?

8. Did it pave the way for something to happen? For a course of action to emerge? For commitment?

9. Did it seem responsible for eventual outcome, or was it merely talk?

10. Did it persuade?

It will be difficult for you to estimate the success of *your* next presentation by using these questions, but you can apply them to the next presentation you attend. Carry this book to the meeting and grade the speaker.

The Checklists

No claim is made for the completeness of these lists, so *add* to them. Their purpose is to try to make you *think* a little bit, and consider a few more things about a presentation than just your mouth.

Checklist A—Things That Are True about Presentations, But Sound Dumb

1. In order to communicate ideas to people we must:
   (a) Have a clearly defined subject
   (b) Select those facts that will make the subject understandable and convincing to the audience
   (c) Arrange the facts and ideas in an effective manner

2. An audience's ability to understand is affected by:
   (a) The vocabulary we choose to use
   (b) The style of presentation
   (c) The way the information is organized
   (d) The general abstractness of the subject
   (e) Idea density

3. Long words are harder to understand than short words.

4. Long sentences are more difficult to understand than short ones.

5. You can't expect to present a lot of ideas in a short period of time. You will bog down in irrelevant details.

6. Presentations are a good idea because people are more apt to act on something they *hear* rather than on something they *read*.

7. When we watch and listen to something we are sensitive to the content, but also to the way the speaker *looks*. And we respond to his manner and delivery.

8. Somebody told me that after a presentation, people will remember about 60 percent of the content. After eight hours they'll remember somewhere between half and a third. (This means that after about seven weeks you'll not only have forgotten the content of this book, you won't even remember where you *put* it.)

Checklist B—Questions to Ask about Your Audience

1. Do they already know something about the subject?
2. Does each individual in the audience know as much as everybody else?
3. Are they interested in the subject?
4. What is their level of understanding?
5. Are there reasons *why* they should be interested?
6. Do they have attitudes about the subject?
7. How much background will you have to provide in order for them to understand the current situation?
8. What are their opinions? About the subject? About the speaker?
9. Has anybody else ever talked to them about it?
10. Is there some way to communicate with them that has been successful in the past?
11. What are their real needs in this case?
12. Will they be able to see connections between what you're saying and what they're doing (living, thinking, or understanding)?
13. Will they be a friendly audience?
14. Will they be open-minded?
15. Are they apt to be hostile?
16. Do you expect them to ask questions?
17. Do you expect them to raise objections?
18. Do you have any idea about the things that might antagonize them? Taboo words? Taboo subjects? Allusions? Something in the past? Gestures?

19. Do they know anything about you?

20. Do they know what level of responsibility or authority you bring to the problem?

21. What is *their* rank? Below, equal with, or higher than yours? Does this have a bearing on your subject matter or style of delivery?

22. Do you think they will expect a formal presentation, or an informal one?

23. Is there anything special about the audience?

24. Is there anything special about the place?

25. Is there anything special about the time (the time of day, week, month, or year)?

26. Is there some connection between you and them?

27. Is there some connection between your organization (company, church, political party) and theirs?

28. What benefits might accrue to *them?*

29. When might they accrue?

30. Are there disadvantages to the audience?

31. What benefits accrue to *you* by addressing this particular audience?

32. Are there *dis*advantages to you?

Checklist C—The Room and Making the Audience Comfortable in It

1. Remember to invite them to the room or the place.

2. Have comfortable chairs to sit in.

3. Arrange the chairs suitably.

4. Make sure that you have the right equipment.

5. Make sure the equipment is in good working order.

6. Make sure that the person operating it isn't a dummy.

7. Assure that there will be a minimum of distractions. (If you're making a presentation in an office, make sure that telephone calls are held.)

8. Provide name cards and place cards when appropriate.

9. Make sure the room has adequate ventilation, particularly when you know that cigar smokers will be present.

10. Make sure the room is suitable from the standpoint of size, number of people in the audience, material to be presented, and so forth. Will the people in the back be able to see?

11. Set aside enough time for breaks. Let people move around, go to the bathroom, etc.

12. Where *are* the bathrooms?

13. See that there are enough electrical outlets, and that they are suitable for the load.

14. Arrange for blackboards and easels.

15. Find a room that is good acoustically. Hard ceilings

and walls reflect sounds and make hearing difficult because of echoes. Curtains and carpeting help.

16. If using projectors, be sure to use a screen and not a wall. Even a white wall will absorb too much light. Beaded screens are best, but they require a certain angle of viewing. (This angle is generally within 20 degrees on either side of the projection axis—which means that half the room will be dead space.)

17. Also, when using projectors allow six square feet per viewer, and don't put anybody closer to the screen than twice the width of the picture. (The viewer should be at least eight feet back from a four-foot picture.)

Checklist D—An Alphabetical List of Items to Remember If You Ever Go Outside Your Own Place

1. acoustics
2. agenda
3. ash trays
4. audiovisual person
5. badges
6. bulletin board in lobby
7. ceiling height
8. chalk
9. checkroom facilities
10. cleanliness
11. coffee breaks
12. confirmations
13. conflicting concurrent meetings
14. cost
15. date of activities
16. direction signs (in lobby and elsewhere)
17. easels
18. entertainment
19. flannel board
20. flip charts
21. floor size
22. hotel reservations
23. lectern (and light)
24. lighting
25. location of windows
26. meal planning and scheduling
27. microphones
28. models and samples
29. name cards
30. optical pointer
31. parking
32. PA system
33. pencils
34. place cards
35. pointer
36. power available
37. projection equipment
38. projection facilities
39. projection personnel
40. recreation
41. registration
42. rest rooms
43. room signs
44. soundproofing
45. spare bulbs for projectors
46. transportation
47. ventilation
48. water pitchers and glasses
49. writing accessories (grease pencils, felt-tip pens)
50. writing pads

Checklist E—Putting Together a New Act

1. Begin by taking the time to write a one-paragraph description of what you intend to do. You may have to answer questions such as, When did the problem start, and why? What are the key parts of the subject matter, and what are the subordinate parts? What is the influence? What is the outlook? How much is involved? How often is it happening?

2. Accumulate data on cards, and spread the cards out in one place so you can see all the key ideas at one time.

3. If no organization becomes immediately apparent, try one of the following systems of presenting information: (a) chronological, (b) cause-and-effect, or (c) problem–solution.

4. At the *beginning* of the presentation you may choose to: (a) acquaint the audience with your qualifications or interests in dealing with the problem, (b) arouse interest in the subject, (c) orient people to the problem, and *(d)* direct attention to some specific issues.

5. In the *middle* of the presentation you might: (a) describe the symptoms of the problem and the influence it seems to be having on people and events, (b) describe the problem, (c) explain the constraints on the solution, (d) summarize various possible solutions, and (e) recommend the best alternative, or combination of alternatives.

6. *End* by summarizing the main ideas, solutions, or opportunities that have emerged in your analysis. Recommend action, even if it is only in the form of further discussion.

7. Go back to point 1. of this checklist and read the first sentence again. That is a very useful idea indeed.

Checklist F—Using Visuals

Common sense will tell you that visuals are used to:

1. Show how things look (as in photos).
2. Show how things work (as in diagrams or models).
3. Show how things relate to each other (as in organization charts).
4. Show important information such as key words or key numbers.

Checklist G—Designing Visuals

1. Use simple terms and relationships.

2. If a visual doesn't explain something better than words, it shouldn't be used.

3. A visual should never exceed forty characters across (counting spaces).

4. It should have a minimum number of lines, certainly no more than eight.

5. Only highlights should be shown.

6. A complete sentence should never be used, only key words or phrases.

7. Cover only one idea per visual, and don't dwell on it for more than a couple of minutes at most.

8. Use a minimum number of curves, never exceeding three.

9. Use a minimum number of grid lines.

10. Eliminate supplementary notes.

11. Omit subtitles.

12. Never use vertical printing.

13. A visual for a presentation should contain far less information than an illustration for a report or a handout.

Checklist H—How to Handle a Group Discussion

1. Develop an outline of the topics to be discussed, and the sensible order in which they should be discussed. Stick to the outline.

2. If such an outline has not been developed ahead of time, begin the discussion by developing one with the audience. Display the ideas prominently on a blackboard or on pages from an easel pad.

3. In case there is insufficient comment, come prepared with appropriate or provocative questions.

4. Don't allow people to get into time-consuming and fruitless arguments.

5. Try to show the relationship of the topics to one another.

6. Try to show the relationship of the topics to objectives.

7. Shut off discussion when a topic has been sufficiently discussed.

8. Try to get participation from everybody present.

9. Encourage members to share experiences or ideas.

10. Don't let one or two people dominate the discussion.

11. Develop a course of action.

12. Prepare for action to take place. Find volunteers to take the next action steps. Failing that, make assignments.

13. Be responsible for the eventual outcome.

Checklist I—What to Make a Presentation *About*

This is a checklist for people who are forced into making a presentation, but don't know what to make it about. It seems ludicrous perhaps to think that such a thing could ever happen to you, but let me assure you that the odds are closer to one-in-two than they are one-in-a-million. The following are guaranteed to work.

1. Talk about the developments in the technology, research, or administration connected with any subject you know about. (To arrive at a title for your presentation, merely take the key subject, add a colon, and attach the words "problems and prospects." It will work for anything: *Tuna Packing: Problems and Prospects*).

2. Talk about problems and solutions (problems with your organization, its goals, its people, its budget, its deadlines, its prospects, etc.).

3. Talk about the *applications* of whatever it is you do, sell, or plan.

4. Talk about innovations made recently. (Or since the beginning of World War II.)

5. Provide instruction about the use of a device, a system, or a concept.

6. Talk about the need for quality control.

7. Talk about new procedures, or invite the audience to help you develop some new procedures.

8. Decide to *evaluate* something. Or somebody. Get audience participation.

9. Formulate a policy or *plan* something.

10. Invite the audience to help you consider some new ways of developing enthusiasm, or improving morale.

Checklist J—Why You Should Rehearse

1. To gain enough familiarity that the right words come out effortlessly and naturally.
2. To allow the easy use of visuals.
3. To look and feel more comfortable.
4. To stay on the track and finish on time.
5. To make it easier for you to answer questions and to anticipate them.
6. Because rehearsal may show up some gaps in your information or holes in your logic.

Checklist K—Using Projection Equipment

1. Make sure it is set up before the event.

2. Make sure that it works.

3. Make sure that it has the right lens.

4. Make sure *you* have the right film or slides.

5. Check the seats (by sitting in them) to make sure that everybody will be able to see.

6. If you need help with the lights, pick somebody ahead of time.

7. After its use, leave the equipment alone until after the entire presentation. Don't bother about rewinding film or putting slides away.

8. Thread the motion picture projector before the event.

9. Prefocus the projector and set the volume level.

10. Have a spare bulb.

11. Know how to change the bulb.

12. Know how to remove a slide that sticks.

13. Remember that sound projectors need time to warm up.

14. Turn off the projector at the end so that people don't have to look at a dazzling white screen.

Checklist L—Grunt Detector

Truth Index

1. Truthful and explicit.
2. A few things didn't ring true.
3. Suspicious.
4. I think you lied and I think they knew it.
5. B.S. and propaganda throughout.

Confusion Scale

1. It was perfectly clear and confused nobody.
2. Once in a while things were a little hard to follow.
3. There were some rough places, such as: _____

_____

_____

4. The whole thing was hazy.
5. I'm afraid it was a fiasco.

Length

1. A little too short. You could have developed some of the ideas a little further.
2. Just right. Everybody felt good.
3. A little long, but O.K.
4. It dragged in a lot of places.
5. Altogether too long. No doubt about it. You spent too much time on: _____

_____

_____

Visuals

1. They were pertinent, easy to see, and easy to understand.
2. They were not always easy to understand.

3. It was hard to see them.
4. They were too complicated.
5. They were unnecessary.

Interest Level

1. Very high. Very interesting at all points.
2. Fascinating in places. Slow in others.
3. Somewhat slow throughout.
4. Rather dull.
5. A real exercise in daylight bombing.

Volume

1. It was O.K. all the time.
2. It was O.K. most of the time.
3. You have some kind of a problem.

Tone of Voice

1. Very natural.
2. As natural as *you* ever get.
3. Spotty.
4. Monotonous as hell.

Diction

1. Every word clear as a bell.
2. A few words were slurred.
3. You may have to give this some serious thought.
4. We should maybe find some kind of a doctor.

Breathing

1. The breathing is O.K.
2. The breathing is not O.K.

Speed and Pacing

1. It went very well. Very natural.

2. There were places where things slowed down, like at: _____

_____

_____

3. There were places where you went a little too fast, like at: _____

_____

_____

4. It was too slow overall.
5. It was too fast overall.

Skill in Phrasing

1. Very good.
2. Pretty good.
3. Fair.
4. Lousy.

General Nervousness

1. Like an actor, already.
2. Some nervousness at the beginning only.
3. Edgy all the way through, but O.K.
4. Nervousness apparent to audience.
5. You looked bad, kid.
6. Get out of show business.

Enthusiasm

1. A little too much.
2. Damned good.
3. Damned average.
4. Marginal.
5. Nonexistent.

Posture

1. Good/natural.

2. You slouched a couple of times.
3. Sloppy.
4. Ludicrous.

General Appearance

1. Great.
2. Snappy.
3. Flashy.
4. Your father took nice care of his clothes.
5. If you're going to wear white socks, then remember to carry a tennis racket.

Facial Expression

1. Good.
2. Indifferent.
3. *What* face?

Eye Contact

1. You looked at everybody. Good.
2. Reasonably good.
3. You tended to look in the same place all the time.
4. Bad. You looked at the floor all the time. (Or you looked at the _____ all the time.)

Gestures

1. Very natural.
2. Generally pretty good.
3. You have trouble with your _____.
4. Weak.
5. You should probably have injections.

Knowledge of Subject

1. Good.
2. Fair.

3. Not so good.
4. Completely out of it.

Delivery

1. You simplified complicated ideas.
2. You complicated simple ideas.
3. I really don't know *what* in the hell you did.

Grammar

1. You've got it.
2. You ain't entirely got it.

It Started Off

1. Great.
2. Slow, but picked up.
3. Slow, but then went to hell.
4. The way it ended. With a thud.

The Language You Used Was

1. Understandable in every case. Appropriate.
2. Confusing in one or two cases.
3. Vague.
4. Too complicated.
5. Lithuanian?

The Presentation Said

1. Quite a bit.
2. Something.
3. Not much.
4. Very little.
5. Nothing new.
6. Nothing at all.

Was It Worth the Time?

1. Yes, well worth it.

2. Yeah, for the most part.
3. I don't know. Half and half.
4. No, quite frankly it wasn't.

Did It Establish Two-Way Communications

1. Sure.
2. Sort of.
3. No.
4. What was the question?

Did It Seem Responsible for Eventual Outcome?

1. Very much.
2. I guess so.
3. I couldn't tell.
4. Obviously not.

Was Anybody Persuaded?

1. All of them.
2. A bunch.
3. A few.
4. One or two.
5. None.
6. One guy said he was going to defect to Albania.

Checklist M—A 22-Point Fantasy

Imagine this. You scheduled a very big and very elaborate series of meetings and presentations. You asked people to fly in from all over. You made every effort you could to persuade them. Two days after the event you receive the following note:

I've never been to a better meeting than yours, and I've stopped to analyze the reasons why I thought it was so good:

1. *It was great, after that long flight, to be met at the airport and not have to worry about luggage, or the hassle of renting a car or finding other transportation.*

2. *It was a pleasant surprise to go into the hotel and be told that I was expected and that registration had already been taken care of.*

3. *The desk clerk handed me the four things you'd prepared: (a) the services and hours of the hotel, (b) the various services (including recreation and entertainment) in the community, (c) a note that explained precisely where I was supposed to go for the first meeting (plus how long it would be and what I could expect), and (d) background information on the speakers and, flatteringly enough, information about us participants.*

4. *It was a nice touch to go to the room and find a small basket of fruit, a couple of good magazines, and a pint of Scotch. It satisfied the three great needs of a late-arriver: a small hunger, boredom, and the need of a drink.*

5. *The room was comfortable, clean, and everything worked.*

6. The hotel food was great and the service excellent.

7. I found the first meeting without any difficulty.

8. The seats were comfortable, and so was the room. It was well ventilated and air conditioned.

9. The meeting started precisely on time, and was run by a person with knowledge and enthusiasm. He set the stage (and the pace) for the rest of the day.

10. I was surprised at how smoothly he used the visuals in his presentation. Usually you have to put up with the noise of a projector, a bumbling projectionist, and a lot of delay getting started. Everything was well organized ahead of time.

11. There were no distractions outside the meeting room. That was a relief. Things went smoothly.

12. Even the coffee break looked like it had been planned like a military operation. It went quickly and smoothly, with no hassles or delays.

13. The arrangement of the room had been worked out so that it was possible to participate and interact (both with the speakers and with other members of the audience).

14. Lunch went well. We were promptly and efficiently served, and had no trouble keeping to the meeting schedule for the afternoon.

15. Rest breaks were conveniently planned throughout the day.

16. It was a good idea to distribute handouts at the end of the sessions. The summaries and outlines will be very useful in remembering what you said.

17. Despite the number of people involved in the pre-

sentations, they were united in purpose and intent. It was well organized.

18. *There were smooth transitions between sessions.*

19. *The presentations were polished and well executed.*

20. *At the end of the day I felt I had participated in something useful and interesting, not merely been subjected to something (or, worse yet, conned).*

21. *There was none of the usual flap at checkout time. You had prearranged everything.*

22. *It was comfortable being taken to the airport.*

I have seldom been treated with as much consideration.